Edward Augustus Freeman

History of the Cathedral Church of Wells

As Illustrating the History of the Cathedral Churches of the Old Foundation

Edward Augustus Freeman

History of the Cathedral Church of Wells
As Illustrating the History of the Cathedral Churches of the Old Foundation

ISBN/EAN: 9783337063276

Printed in Europe, USA, Canada, Australia, Japan

Cover: Foto ©ninafisch / pixelio.de

More available books at **www.hansebooks.com**

HISTORY

OF THE

CATHEDRAL CHURCH OF WELLS.

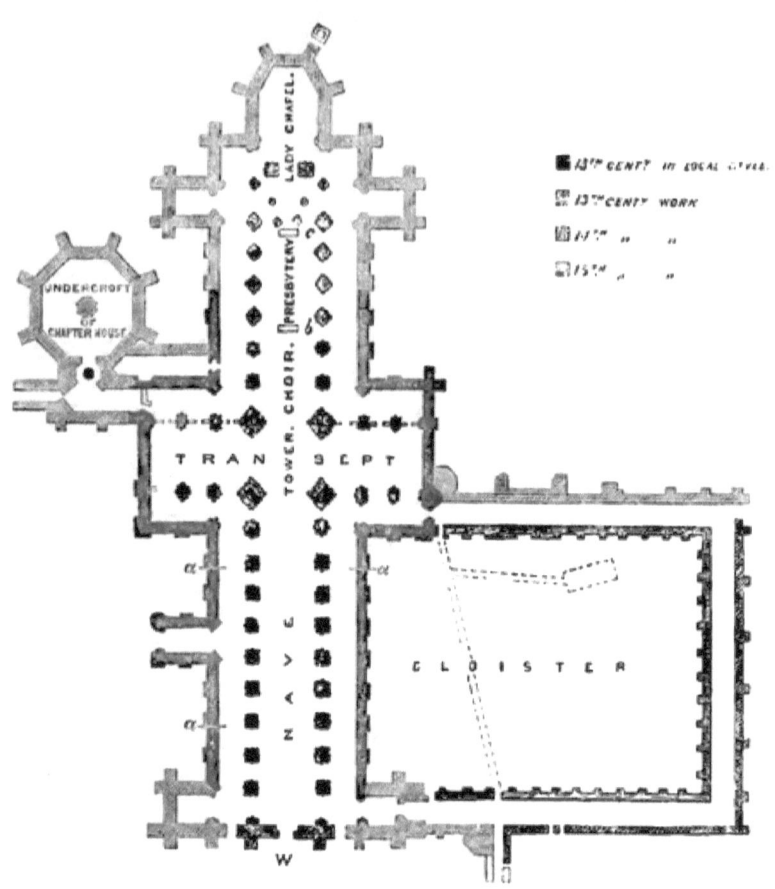

HISTORY OF

THE

CATHEDRAL CHURCH

Of Wells

AS

ILLUSTRATING THE HISTORY OF

THE CATHEDRAL CHURCHES

OF THE

OLD FOUNDATION.

BY

EDWARD A. FREEMAN, M.A.

FORMERLY FELLOW OF TRINITY COLLEGE, OXFORD.

London:
MACMILLAN AND CO.
1870.

LONDON:
R. CLAY, SONS, AND TAYLOR, PRINTERS,
BREAD STREET HILL.

CONTENTS.

	PAGE
	1
	42
	105
	163
	191

PREFACE.

THIS small volume is a reprint, with hardly any change, of three lectures which were given to a local society in Wells in the months of December 1869 and January 1870, and which were printed at the time in a local paper. I have added some notes and references, but the substance is essentially the same. The subject seemed to deserve more than local attention on more grounds than one. I wished to point out the way in which local and general history may and ought to be brought together. As a general rule, local historians make hardly any attempt to connect the history of the particular church or city or district of which they are writing with the general history of the country, or even with the general history of its own class of institutions. On the other hand, more general students of history are apt to pay too little heed to the history of particular places. I have here tried to treat the history of the Church of Wells as a contribution to the general history of the Church and Kingdom of England, and specially to the history of the Cathedral Churches of the Old Foundation. I have also a special object in calling attention to the origin and history of those foundations, to their original objects and their modern corruptions. It is quite impossible that our Cathedral institutions can stay much longer in the state in which they now are, a state which satisfies no party. If they are not reformed by their friends, they can hardly fail to be destroyed by their enemies. The awkward attempt at reform which was made thirty years back was made in utter ignorance of the history and nature of the institutions. Instead of reforming them, it has merely crippled them. Our Cathedral Churches have indeed vastly improved during those thirty years; but it has been almost wholly because they have shared in a general improvement, hardly at all by virtue of the changes which were specially meant to improve them. I wish to point out the general principles of the original founders as the model to which the Old Foundations should be brought back, and the New Foundations reformed after their pattern.

What I have now written is of course a mere sketch, which does not at all pretend to be a complete history of the Church of Wells, either architectural or documentary. I had hoped that Professor Willis would have allowed me the use of the materials of both kinds on which he grounded his lectures in 1851 and 1863. But it seems that he reserves them for the general work for which architectural students have been waiting so long. I have therefore been left to my own resources, that is, as far as documents are concerned, to the ordinary printed authorities in *Anglia Sacra*, the *Monasticon*, and elsewhere. But it is to be hoped that some day or other the documents that are locked up in manuscript at Wells and at other places may be made available for historical purposes. Some of our capitular records would be excellently suited for a place in the series issued by the Master of the Rolls.

I have given an historical ground-plan, but the scale of the book forbade any strictly architectural illustrations, while it seemed needless to give any mere picturesque views of a building of which engravings and photographs are so common.

SOMERLEAZE, WELLS,
May 18th, 1870.

LIST OF BISHOPS.

BISHOPS OF SOMERSETSHIRE OR WELLS.

	Consecration.	Death or Translation.
Æthelhelm	909	914[1]
Wulfhelm	914	923[1]
Ælfheah	923	937 ?
Wulfhelm	938	955 ?
Brihthelm	956	973
Cyneward	973	975
Sigar	975	997
Ælfwine	997	998 ?
Lyfing	999	1012[1]
Æthelwine } [2]	1013	1023 ?
Brihtwine }	1013	1023 ?
Merewith	1027	1033
Duduc	1033	1060
Gisa	1061	1088

BISHOPS OF BATH.

	Consecration or Translation.	Death or Translation.
John de Villulâ	1088	1122
Godfrey	1123	1135
Robert	1136	1166
Reginald	1174	1191[3]

(1) Translated to Canterbury.
(2) This seems to have been a case of disputed election.
(3) Translated to Canterbury.

BISHOP OF BATH AND GLASTONBURY.

	Consecration or Translation.	Death or Translation.
Savaric	1192	1205

BISHOPS OF BATH AND WELLS.

	Consecration or Translation.	Death or Translation.
Jocelin of Wells	1206	1242
Roger	1244	1247
William Button	1248	1264
Walter Giffard	1265	1266 [1]
William Button	1267	1274
Robert Burnell	1275	1292
William of March	1293	1302
Walter Hasleshaw	1302	1308
John Drokensford	1309	1329
Ralph of Shrewsbury	1329	1363
John Barnet	1363 [2]	1366 [3]
John Harewell	1367	1386
Walter Skirlaw	1386 [4]	1388 [5]
Ralph Erghum	1388 [6]	1400
Henry Bowett	1401	1407 [7]
Nicholas Bubwith	1407 [8]	1424
John Stafford	1425	1443 [9]
Thomas Beckington	1443	1465
Robert Stillington	1466	1491
Richard Fox	1492 [10]	1494 [11]

(1) Translated to York.
(2) Translated from Worcester.
(3) Translated to Ely.
(4) Translated from Coventry and Lichfield.
(5) Translated to Durham.
(6) Translated from Salisbury.
(7) Translated to York.
(8) Translated from London to Salisbury, and thence to Bath and Wells.
(9) Translated to Canterbury.
(10) Translated from Exeter.
(11) Translated to Durham, thence to Winchester.

LIST OF BISHOPS.

	Consecration or Translation.	Death or Translation.
Oliver King	1495[1]	1503
Hadrian de Castello	1504[2]	1518[3]
Thomas Wolsey	1518[4]	1523[5]
John Clark	1523	1541
William Knight	1541	1547
William Barlow	1549[6]	1554[7]
Gilbert Bourne	1554	1559[8]
Gilbert Berkeley	1560	1581
Thomas Godwin	1584	1590[9]
John Still	1593	1608
James Montague	1608	1616[10]
Arthur Lake	1616	1626
William Laud	1626[11]	1628[12]
Leonard Mawe	1628	1629
Walter Curll	1629[13]	1632[14]
William Piers	1632[15]	1670
Robert Creighton	1670	1672
Peter Mews	1673	1684[16]
Thomas Ken	1685	1690[17]
Richard Kidder	1691	1703
George Hooper	1704[18]	1727
John Wynne	1727[18]	1743

(1) Translated from Exeter.
(2) Translated from Hereford.
(3) Deprived for a conspiracy against Pope Leo the Tenth.
(4) Held in plurality with York.
(5) Exchanged for Durham.
(6) Translated from Saint David's.
(7) Deprived on the accession of Queen Mary and reappointed to Chichester under Queen Elizabeth.
(8) Deprived on the accession of Elizabeth.
(9) Father of Francis Godwin the historian, Canon of Wells and afterwards Bishop of Llandaff.
(10) Translated to Winchester.
(11) Translated from Saint David's.
(12) Translated to London and thence to Canterbury.
(13) Translated from Rochester.
(14) Translated to Winchester.
(15) Translated from Peterborough.
(16) Translated to Winchester.
(17) Deprived for refusing the oaths to William and Mary.
(18) Translated from Saint Asaph.

	Consecration or Translation.	Death or Translation.
Edward Willis	1743[1]	1773
Charles Moss	1774[1]	1802
Richard Beadon	1802[2]	1824
George Henry Law	1824[3]	1845
Hon. Richard Bagot	1845[4]	1854
Robert John Lord Auckland	1854[5]	1869[6]
Lord Arthur Charles Hervey	1869	

[1] Translated from Saint David's.
[2] Translated from Gloucester.
[3] Translated from Carlisle.
[4] Translated from Oxford.
[5] Translated from Sodor and Man.
[6] Resigned. Died 1870.

HISTORY

OF THE

CATHEDRAL CHURCH OF WELLS.

LECTURE I.

THE subject which I have chosen for this course of lectures is one which must always have an interest beyond all others for us who live in this city and neighbourhood. In every place which boasts of a cathedral church, that cathedral church is commonly the chief object of interest, alike as its present ornament and as the chief centre of its past history. But in Wells the cathedral church and its appurtenances are yet more. Their interest is not only primary, but absorbing. They are not only the chief ornament of the place; they are the place itself. They are not only the centre of the past history of the city; their history is the history of the city. Of our other cities some can trace up a long history as cities independent of their ecclesiastical foundations. Some were the dwelling-places of Kings in days before England became one kingdom. Some have been for ages seats of commerce or manufactures; their history is the history of burghers striving for and obtaining their freedom, a history which repeats in small that same tale of early struggles and later abuses which forms the history of so many greater commonwealths. Others have a long military history; their name at once suggests the memory of battles and sieges, and they can still show walls and castles as the living memorials of the stirring scenes of bygone times. In others even the ecclesiastical pre-eminence of the cathedral church may be disputed by some other ecclesiastical building. The bishoprick and its church may be comparatively modern institutions, and they may be altogether eclipsed by some other institution more ancient in date of foundation, perhaps more ancient in its actual fabric. Thus at Oxford the cathedral church is well-nigh lost among the buildings of the University and its greatest college. At Chester its rank may be disputed by the majestic fragments of the older minster of Saint John. At Bristol the cathedral church, even when restored to its old proportions, will still have at least an equal rival in the stateliest parish church in England. In these cities the bishoprick, its church and its chapter, are institutions of yesterday; the cities themselves were great and famous for ages before they were founded. So at Exeter, though the bishoprick is of far earlier date, yet Exeter was a famous city, which had played its part in history, long before Bishops of Exeter were heard of. Even at Winchester the overwhelming greatness of the Old Minster has to compete with the earlier and later interests of the royal palace, of the fallen Abbey, of the unique home of noble poverty ([1]) and of the oldest

([1]) See notes at the end of the volume.

of the great and still living schools of England. Salisbury alone in our own part of England, and Durham in the far north, have a history which in some measure resembles that of Wells. Like Wells, Salisbury and Durham are cities which have grown up around the cathedral church. But they have grown up—I presume it is no offence to say so—into a greater measure of temporal importance than our own city. To take a familiar standard, no one has ever proposed to strike either of them out of the list of parliamentary boroughs. Wells stands alone among the cities of England proper as a city which exists only in and through its cathedral church, whose whole history is that of its cathedral church. The Bishoprick has been to us what the Abbey has been to our neighbours at Glastonbury, what the church first of Abbots and then of Bishops has been elsewhere to Ely and Peterborough. The whole history of Wells is, I say, the history of the bishoprick and of its church. Of the origin and foundation of the city, as distinguished from that of the church, nothing is known. The name of Wells is first heard of as the place where the church of Saint Andrew was standing, and its name seldom appears in later history except in connexion with the affairs of its church. It was never a royal dwelling-place; it was never a place of commercial importance; it was never a place of military strength. Like other cities, it has its municipal history, but its municipal history is simply an appendage to its ecclesiastical history; the franchises of the borough were simply held as grants from the Bishop. It has its parochial church, a church standing as high among the buildings of its own class as the cathedral church itself. This parochial church has a parochial constitution which is in some points unique. But the parochial church is simply an appendage to the cathedral church; it is the church of the burghers who had come to dwell under the shadow of the minster and the protection of its spiritual lord. And it has ever retained a close, sometimes perhaps a too close, connexion with the cathedral and its Chapter. Thus the history of the church is the history of the city; no battles, no sieges, no parliaments, break the quiet tenor of its way; the name of the city has hardly found its way into our civil and military history. Its name does appear among the troubles of the seventeenth century, in the pages of Clarendon and of Macaulay, but it appears in connexion with events whose importance was mainly local. And even here the ecclesiastical interest comes in; the most striking event connected with Wells in the story of Monmouth's rebellion is the mischief done to the cathedral, and the way in which further damage and desecration was hindered by Lord Grey. And in our own times, when the parliamentary existence of this city became the subject of an animated parliamentary discussion, even then the ecclesiastical interest was still uppermost. The old battle of the regulars and seculars was fought again over the bodies of two small parliamentary boroughs. I need not remind you that the claims of the old secular foundation were stoutly pressed by one of our own members. But the monastic influence was too strong for us; the mantle of Dunstan and Æthelwald had fallen on the shoulders of Sir John Pakington, and the claims of the fallen Abbey of Evesham were preferred to those of the existing Cathedral of Wells.(²)

The whole interest, then, of this city is ecclesiastical; but its ecclesiastical interest in one point of view surpasses that of every church in England,—I am strongly tempted to say, every church in Europe. The traveller who comes down the hill from Shepton Mallet looks down, as he draws near the city, on a group of buildings which, as far as I know, has no rival either in our own island or beyond the sea. To most of these objects, taken singly, it would be easy to find rivals which would equal or surpass them. The church itself, seen even from that most favourable point of view, cannot, from mere lack of bulk, hold its ground against the soaring apse of Amiens, or against the windows ranging, tier above tier, in the mighty eastern gable of Ely. The cloister cannot measure itself with Gloucester or Salisbury; the chapter-house lacks the soaring roofs of York and Lincoln; the palace itself finds its rival in the ruined pile of Saint David's. The peculiar charm and glory of Wells lies in the union and harmonious grouping of all. The church does not stand alone; it is neither crowded by incongruous buildings, nor yet isolated from those buildings which are its natural and necessary complement. Palace, cloister, Lady chapel, choir, chapter-house, all join to form one indivisible whole. The series goes on uninterruptedly along that unique bridge which by a marvel of ingenuity connects the church itself with the most perfect of buildings of its own class, the matchless Vicars' close.

Scattered around we see here and there an ancient house, its gable, its window, or its turret falling in with the style and group of greater buildings, and bearing its part in producing the general harmony of all. The whole history of the place is legibly written on that matchless group of buildings. If we could fancy an ecclesiastical historian to have dropped from the clouds, the aspect of the place would at once tell him that he was looking on an English cathedral church, on a cathedral church which had always been served by secular canons, on a church of secular canons which had preserved its ancient buildings and ancient arrangements more perfectly than any other in the island. It is to the history of that great institution, alike in its fabric and its foundation, that I call your attention in the present course of lectures. And, taking Wells as my text, I purpose to compare our own church, alike in its fabric and its foundation, with other churches of the same class. The subject naturally falls into three divisions. I purpose to devote three discourses of moderate length to the early, the mediæval, and the modern history of the Church of Wells.

For a subject like that which I have chosen is obviously one which may be looked at from various points of view. A cathedral church like ours is not only a material fabric, a work of architecture; it is also an ecclesiastical institution, an establishment founded for the benefit of our Church and nation, and which has played its part, whatever that part may have been, in the general history of the country. I purpose to look at it in both aspects, aspects either of which is very imperfectly treated if it wholly shuts out the other. But I do not purpose to treat either branch of the subject in any very minute detail. A minute architectural or antiquarian memoir has its value, but it is not at all suited to a popular lecture. A minute architectural exposition, if it is to be intelligible, must be given on the spot. A minute antiquarian memoir, crowded with names and dates, is often very profitable when printed, but it is not at all suited to be read out to a general audience. Moreover I should be very sorry to trespass on the province of one to whose minute knowledge of local history I can make no claim. My object is different. I wish to treat the history of Wells Cathedral, both as a building and as an institution, in a more general, in what I may call a comparative, way. I wish to dwell on the position of our own church as one of a class, to point out how it stands among other buildings and other institutions of its own class, and to trace out its connexion with the general history of the Kingdom and Church of England.

For my first portion then this evening, I purpose to take as my subject the early days of the church of Saint Andrew, from the first time that its name is heard of in history or record to the time when both the material fabric and the ecclesiastical foundation assumed something like their present form. And as this subject will lead us into somewhat obscure times, and into many matters which people in general are far from accurately understanding, I hope that those among my hearers to whom all that I have to say is familiar will forgive me if I deal with some matters in a somewhat elementary way. I have spoken of Saint Andrew's church in Wells as a cathedral church, as a cathedral church which has always been served by secular canons; I have spoken of an opposition between the regular and the secular clergy. To some of my hearers all these terms carry their meaning at once. To others I am afraid that they may not suggest any very definite idea. But without a definite idea of them neither the general history of England nor the local history of Wells can be clearly understood. Let then my better informed hearers bear with me if I go somewhat into the A B C of the matter.

To begin then with the beginning, what do we mean when we call the larger of the two ancient churches in this city, the *Cathedral?* What is the meaning of the word? Some people seem to think it means simply a bigger church than usual—I have heard a vast number of churches in other places called *cathedrals* which have no right to the name. Sometimes people seem to think that it means a church which has a Dean and Chapter or a special body of clergy of some kind, or a church where there are prayers every day, or a church where the prayers are chanted and not merely read. Nay, some people seem to think that a cathedral is not a church at all; I have heard it said that a cathedral was not a church, but that it had a church inside it. And I do not wonder at people thinking so when they go into a cathedral church, and see the greater part standing empty indeed and swept, but never garnished. I was once in a large parish church, that of Grosmont in Monmouthshire, where the man who let me in told me very proudly: "Our church is like a cathedral." What he meant by the church being like a cathedral was that the whole congregation was rammed, jammed, crammed into the choir, while the nave stood empty and useless. Again it is not at all uncommon to hear people talk of "cathedrals and churches," as if they were two different sorts of things. And people seem also to think that some particular sort of worship is right in a cathedral, which is not right in other places. When there is a good deal of singing and organ-playing in divine service, they call it "cathedral service," as if singing and organ-playing were something specially belonging to a cathedral more than to other places.

Now all these latter notions are simply mistakes. And those with which I began are mistakes too, though in a somewhat different way. A cathedral is simply a church, one particular sort of church, and, instead of being a thing to be proud of, it is a thing to be ashamed of if the nave of any church stands empty and useless. What is called "cathedral service" is simply divine service done in the best and most solemn way, a way which other churches may not always be able to follow in everything, but which they should try to follow as nearly as they can. On the other hand, it is very right that a cathedral church should be larger and finer than other churches, that it should have a larger body of clergy belonging to it, and that they should perform divine service in such a way as to be a light and an example to other churches. Still none of these things lies at the root of the matter; it is none of these things which makes the difference between a cathedral and another church. That difference is that it contains the throne or official seat of the Bishop. In Greek and Latin that seat is called *cathedra*,—a word which in English is cut short into *chair*—and the church which contains it is called *ecclesia cathedralis*, the *cathedral church*. *Cathedral* in short is an adjective and not a substantive, and its use as a substantive is always rather awkward and slovenly. Certain churches, namely those which contain the throne of a Bishop, are *cathedral* churches, as churches which do not contain the throne of a Bishop, but which have a Chapter or College of clergy, are *collegiate* churches, while the great mass of churches are simply *parochial* churches, churches designed for the use of a single parish, and with only a single parish priest.

The essence then of the cathedral church is its being, beyond all other churches, the church of the Bishop. It is the church which contains his official seat, and it is by taking possession of that official seat that the Bishop, as we shall presently see when our newly chosen Bishop comes among us, takes possession of his Bishoprick.([3]) From that seat the church, and the city in which it stands, is called the Bishop's *See*. And from that see the Bishop takes his title. Thus we call this city of Wells the see of a Bishop, the Bishop of Bath and Wells. The Bishop is called Bishop of Bath as well as of Wells, because this diocese, unlike most others, contained two cathedral churches. The Bishop had his throne in the church of Saint Peter at Bath as well as in the church of Saint Andrew at Wells. But since the time of Henry the Eighth the church of Bath has not been reckoned as a cathedral church, and the Bishop has been enthroned in the church of Wells only.

Now you may ask how it is that, while, of all the churches of the diocese, the cathedral church is preeminently the Bishop's church, the church which is specially his own, and whence he takes his title, it is precisely in the cathedral church that he has less authority than in any other church, that the whole management of the cathedral church seems to have passed away from the Bishop into the hands of the Dean and Chapter. The independence of the Dean and Chapter, when it is carried so far as it now is, is undoubtedly an abuse and an anomaly, and how it came about I shall show as I go on. You may also ask how it happened that the see of the Bishop of this diocese should have been placed at Wells rather than anywhere else. For it was at Wells that it was placed first of all, and it was not till nearly two hundred years after the foundation of the Bishoprick that Bath became a cathedral church.

To see how this happened we must go back to the days of the first preaching of the Gospel to Englishmen. In those parts of Western Europe which first became Christian, in Italy, for instance, and Gaul and Spain, the cities were at that time almost everything; the open country was of very little account. The Gospel was therefore first preached to the people of the cities, and the cities had become almost wholly Christian at a time when the people of the country were still mainly heathens. Hence the word *pagan*— in Latin *paganus*—which at first meant only a countryman as opposed to a townsman, came to mean a heathen or worshipper of false gods. Now in this state of things the Bishop was pre-eminently the Bishop of the city; the city was his home, and the home of his original flock; it was only gradually that he came to have much to do with the people beyond the city, and, when he did so, the limits of his diocese were fixed by the limits of the civil jurisdiction of the city of which he was Bishop. In England, and indeed in the British Islands generally, the state of things was very different. The country was divided among many princes; there were but few large towns, and those that there were exercised no authority over the people of the country round them. In England therefore at first there commonly was a Bishop in each Kingdom; he fixed his throne, his *bishopstool* as it was called, in some particular church in his diocese, which thus became his special home and cathedral church; but he was not Bishop of the city in the same special sense in which an Italian or even a Gaulish Bishop was Bishop of the city. In fact in many of the English dioceses the Bishop did not even take his title from the city where his cathedral church stood, but was called from the country at large, or rather from the tribe which inhabited it. Thus up to the Norman Conquest the Bishop of this diocese was not called the Bishop of Wells, but the Bishop of the Sumorsætas, the tribe from which Somersetshire takes its name.

Now the Bishoprick of the Sumorsætas was not one of the oldest Bishopricks, one of those which were founded at the first preaching of the Gospel in England. When Augustine came to Britain in 597, only a very small part of Somersetshire was English at all; the Welsh of Cornwall still held all the land from the Land's End to the Axe. Thus Wells, if Wells existed, was within the Welsh border, though Wookey was within the English border. When the West-Saxons became Christians in 635, a Bishop was, as usual, appointed for the whole kingdom. He was called Bishop of the West-Saxons, and his *bishopstool* was placed, after some changes, in the royal city of Winchester.([1]) After a while, as Christianity spread and as the West-Saxon Kingdom grew by conquests from the Welsh, this great diocese was divided in the year 705.([5]) One Bishop remained at Winchester; the other had his *bishopstool* at Sherborne, and his diocese took in the shires of the Dorsætas, the Wilsætas, and the Sumorsætas, and Berkshire, a shire which, unlike the other three, was not called after a people. In the time of Eadward the Elder, in 909, this diocese was divided again; the Sumorsætas now got a Bishop to themselves, and his *bishopstool* was placed where it still is, in the church of Saint Andrew at Wells.([6])

Now we come at once to the question, why was Wells chosen to be the seat of the Bishoprick? I think you will easily see that there is not now, nor was there then, any diocese in England where the Bishop was more thoroughly driven to be the Bishop of the whole diocese and not merely the Bishop of one city. Somersetshire had not then, and it has not now, any one town at once larger than any of its neighbours and placed conveniently in the middle of the shire. Then, as now, the two greatest towns in the shire must have been the old Roman city of Bath at

one end and the purely English town of Taunton at
the other. Taunton was founded by King Ine between
710 and 722 as a border fortress against the Welsh,
after he had carried the English frontier as far west as
the boundary of Somersetshire goes now.(⁷) Neither
of these places was well suited to be the centre of the
diocese. Bridgewater, which is more central, was not
built till some ages later. Glastonbury, which is more
central still, could not well be made the Bishoprick,
because it was the seat of the greatest monastery of
the West. Also Glastonbury was in those days a
singularly inaccessible place. It stood on an island,
and could be reached only by boats; so that unless
the Bishop was to be altogether a hermit, he would
have been a good deal out of place there. Some
Bishops had fixed their sees in places of this kind,
but it is clear that such an arrangement was in every
way inconvenient, and so wise a King as Eadward the
Elder was not likely to sanction it. And we may be
sure that the monks of Glastonbury would be then,
as they were long after, altogether set against having
the Bishop for their chief instead of an Abbot of their
own. I conceive that Wells was chosen, because at
Wells there was already a body of secular priests
attached to the church of Saint Andrew.

The whole history of Wells before the time of
Eadward the Elder is excessively obscure, and much
of it is undoubtedly fabulous. There is a story about
King Ine planting a Bishoprick at Congresbury, which
was presently moved to Wells, and a list of Bishops
is given between Ine and Eadward. There is also a
document which professes to be a charter of King

Cynewulf in 766, which does not speak of any Bishop at Wells, but which implies the existence of an ecclesiastical establishment of some kind. But unluckily the Congresbury story rests on no good authority, and the charter of Cynewulf is undoubtedly spurious. But because a charter is spurious in form, it does not always follow that its matter is unhistorical. And I am the more inclined to attach some value to it, because, while implying the existence of some ecclesiastical establishment, it does not imply the existence of a Bishoprick. Putting all things together, and remembering the strong and consistent tradition which connects the name of Ine with the church of Wells, I am inclined to think that there must have been some body of priests, probably of Ine's foundation, existing at Wells before the foundation of the Bishoprick by Eadward.([8]) If then Ine did, somewhere about the year 705, found a church at Wells with a body of priests attached to it, we can well understand why Wells should be chosen as the seat of the new Bishoprick in 909. The secular canons of Ine's foundation could receive the Bishop as their chief, and become his *Chapter*, in a way in which the monks of Glastonbury could not so well do. If this be so, then the Chapter of Wells is really an older institution than the Bishoprick. The present form of the Chapter is, as I shall presently show, comparatively modern; but if this be so, the priests of Wells are, in one shape or another, two hundred years older than the Bishop. On this view, Eadward the Elder did with the church of Wells exactly what has been done with the churches of Ripon and Manchester in our own time. Both these churches were *collegiate;* Ripon had a Dean and Prebendaries; Manchester had a Warden and Fellows. In our present Queen's reign Bishopricks were founded in these two churches; from being only *collegiate*, they became *cathedral*, and the collegiate bodies became the Chapters of the new Bishops. In the like sort it seems probable that the church of Saint Andrew at Wells, founded by King Ine as a collegiate church, was made into a cathedral church by King Eadward the Elder. Saint Andrew's church therefore may be said to have two founders; King Ine founded the Chapter, King Eadward founded the Bishoprick. Now perhaps some of you read the notice which was placed on the choir-door last week summoning all the members of the Chapter to attend for the election of the new Bishop. You might there have seen the Queen's *congé d'élire*, the writ giving leave to the Chapter to elect a Bishop. In that *congé d'élire*, the Queen calls her rights over the church of Wells her "fundatorial rights." That is to say, they are the rights which she has inherited as the successor of King Ine, as not only the successor but the direct descendant of King Eadward the Elder.

Let us now try and picture to ourselves the state of things at Wells and in its neighbourhood at either of these early times. In some respects the aspect of the country has greatly changed; in others closely connected with them the influence of the then state of things abides to this day. The traveller who in Ine's day looked down from the height of Mendip looked down on a land which had been but lately wrested from its old British owners. By the hard fighting of about a hundred and twenty years the English border had been carried from the Axe to nearly the present limits of the shire.(9) Taunton was a border fortress, newly raised against the gradually retreating but still often threatening Welsh. If the eye caught the hills of Devon or perhaps even those of Western Somerset, it looked, no less than when it looked across the Channel to the hills of Gwent and Morganwg, upon a foreign and hostile land.(10) The great natural features of the country were of course the same as they are now. The rocks of Cheddar and of Ebber, the bold headland of Brean, the island rock of the Steep Holm, the little hills scattered here and there, and the knoll of Brent and the Tor of the Archangel rising above their fellows, are objects which do not change. But in the days of Ine we must remember that those hills were truly islands. The low ground was one wide extent of marsh; the dwelling-places of man were confined to those ridges and isolated heights where the ground was high enough to be safe against accidents of tide and flood. Mendip itself was a wild forest land, peopled only by beasts of chase, and we must remember that the hunters of those days had to struggle against really formidable foes. The cave-lion had indeed long ago vanished, but we cannot doubt that the wolf still preyed on the flocks, and that the wild boar still ravaged the fields, of the men who were striving to bring the land into subjection. The inhabitants were doubtless still mainly of the old British stock, no longer dealt with as wild beasts or as irreclaimable enemies, but allowed to sit down as subjects, though as subjects of an inferior class, under the rule of the West-Saxon King.([11]) But English influence was fast spreading; between the days of Ine and the days of Eadward the tongue and laws and manners of the conquerors had spread themselves, and, by the time of the second foundation of Wells, Somersetshire must have been mainly an English land. The evidence of nomenclature shows us that most of the sites now occupied, most of the old towns and villages, were occupied between these two dates, and the population must have been, then as now, thickly scattered over the insular and peninsular heights of the district. I need not tell you that it is mainly along those old lines of habitation that men dwell still. Along the hill-sides of Mendip and of the opposite ridges villages and houses lie thick together, while the flat land below, though it has become the wealth of the country, remains almost as little dwelled in by man as in the days when it was one impassable swamp. And in the land which was thus fast becoming part of the inheritance of Englishmen, the piety and discernment of English Kings had planted two special centres of religion and civilization, richly endowed of the wealth of the land for the common benefit of all. In the isle of Avalon, the isle of Glastonbury, the great Abbey still lived on, rich and favoured by the conquerors as by the conquered, the one great institution which bore up untouched through the storm of English Conquest, the one great tie which binds our race to the race which went before us, and which binds the Church of the last thirteen hundred years to the earlier days of Christianity in Britain. There in their island monks and pilgrims still worshipped in that primæval church of wood and wicker which time and conquest had as yet agreed to spare.(¹²) To the north of the old British monastery, not alone on an island, but nestling under the shadow of the great hill range itself, the younger ecclesiastical foundation, the foundation of the conquerors, was growing up. Of purely English and Christian origin, claiming no Roman or British forerunner, the church and town which were rising at the foot of Mendip drew their name from no legend of old times, from no tradition of gods and heroes, but from the most marked natural feature of the spot and from the patron saint in whose name the young foundation was hallowed. While the origin of the Abbey is lost in the gloom of hoariest antiquity, while its name of Avalon has become a name of legend, a name rather of some fancied fairy-land than of an actual spot of earth, no traditions, no legends, have decorated the birth and early years of the church and city which drew its name, as intelligible to English ears now as it was then, from the holy wells of Saint Andrew.

Two ecclesiastical foundations, two centres of civilization, were thus planted in each other's near neighbourhood; but it is the history of one only of them with which we are now concerned. I have not to follow out the tale of the monks of Glastonbury, but that of the secular priests of Wells. And here perhaps it may be needful to set forth more fully the exact meaning of those words, and to say something about the two different classes of clergy in those days, the differences between whom tore the whole country in pieces at a time a little later than the foundation of our Bishoprick. Some people seem to fancy that all the clergy in old times were monks. I have heard people talk of monks even in our church of Wells, where there never was a monk. Indeed they sometimes seem to fancy that not only all the clergy but all mankind were monks; at least one hardly ever sees an old house, be it parsonage or manor-house or any other, but some one is sure to tell us that monks once lived in it. It is hard to make people understand that there were clergymen in those days, just as there are now, parsons of parishes and canons of cathedral or collegiate churches, living, as they do now, in their own houses, and in early times not uncommonly married. These were the *secular* clergy, the clergy who live in the world. The monks, on the other hand, the *regular* clergy, those who live according to rule, were originally men who, instead of living in the world to look after the souls of others, went out of the world to look after their own souls. There is no need that a monk should be a priest, or that he should be in holy orders at all, and the first monks were all laymen. Gradually however the monks took holy orders, and they did much good in many places by teaching and civilizing the people, by preaching and writing books, and, not least, by tilling the ground. But in all this they were rather forsaking their own proper duty as monks and taking on them the duty of secular priests. The main difference between them came to be that the monks bound themselves by three vows, those of poverty, chastity, and obedience, while the secular clergy did not take vows, but were simply bound, as they are now, to obey whatever might be the law of the Church at the time. Now of these two classes of clergy some of our early Kings and Bishops preferred one and some the other. But whenever a new diocese was founded, the Bishop surrounded himself with a company of clergy of one sort or the other. You will remember that when a bishoprick, say that of the West-Saxons, was founded, the cathedral church was the first church that was built and endowed. The Bishop of the West-Saxons had his home at Winchester, along with a body of monks or clergy, who were his special companions and advisers, his helpers in keeping up divine worship in the cathedral church, and in spreading the Gospel in other parts of the diocese. Gradually churches and monasteries were built in other places, and monks and clergy were appointed to serve them, but a special body of monks or clergy always remained at the cathedral church, to be the Bishop's special companions, and to keep up the cathedral church as the model and example for the whole diocese. This is the origin of the Chapters of our cathedral churches. The clergy of a cathedral were sometimes regulars and sometimes seculars; and as men looked on the monks as holier than the seculars, the seculars were turned out of several cathedral and other churches, and monks were put in their place. Hence several of our cathedrals were served by monks down to the time of Henry the Eighth, when all monasteries were suppressed, and the cathedral monasteries, as at Canterbury, Winchester, and elsewhere, were changed into chapters of secular canons. But in other churches, as in our own church of Wells, and in the neighbouring churches of Exeter and Salisbury, the secular canons have always gone on to this day. And this makes a great difference in the appearance of our buildings at Wells from those of many other cities. We have here in Wells the finest collection of domestic buildings surrounding a cathedral church to be seen anywhere. There is no place where so many ancient houses are preserved and are mainly applied to their original uses. The Bishop still lives in the Palace; the Dean still lives in the Deanery; the Canons, Vicars, and other officers still live very largely in the houses in which they were meant to live. But this is because at Wells there always were secular priests, each man living in his own house. In a monastery I need hardly say it was quite different. The monks did not live each man in his own house; they lived in common, with a common refectory to dine in and a common dormitory to sleep in. Thus when, in Henry the Eighth's time, the monks were put out and secular canons put in again, the monastic buildings were no longer of any use, while there were no houses for the new canons. They had therefore to make houses how they could out of the common buildings of the monastery. But of course this could not be done without greatly spoiling them as works of architecture. Thus while at Ely, Peterborough, and other churches which were served by monks, there are still very fine fragments of the monastic buildings, there is not the same series of buildings each still applied to its original use which we have at Wells. I wish that this wonderful series was better understood and more valued than it is. I can remember, if nobody else does, how a fine prebendal hall was wantonly pulled down in the North Liberty not many years ago. Some of those whose duty it was to keep it up said that they had never seen it. I had seen it, anybody who went by could see it, and every man of taste knew and regretted it. Well, that is gone, and I suppose the organist's house, so often threatened, will soon be gone too. Thus it is that the historical monuments of our country perish day by day. We must keep a sharp eye about us or this city of ours may lose, almost without anybody knowing it, the distinctive character which makes it unique among the cities of England.

It is then in this way that Wells became, what it still is, the seat of the Somersetshire Bishoprick. The Bishop had his throne in the church of Saint Andrew, and the clergy attached to that church were his special companions and advisers, in a word his Chapter. We have thus the church and its ministers, but the church had not yet assumed its present form, and its ministers had not yet assumed their present constitution. Of the fabric, as it stood in the tenth century, I can tell you nothing. There is not a trace of building of anything like such early date remaining: while in other places we have grand buildings of the eleventh and twelfth centuries, at Wells we have little or nothing earlier than the thirteenth. But it is quite a mistake to fancy that our forefathers in the tenth century were wholly incapable of building, or that their buildings were always of wood. We have accounts of churches of that and of still earlier date which show that we had then buildings of considerable size and elaboration of plan.(13) And we know that in the course of the same century Saint Dunstan built a stone church at Glastonbury to the east of the old wooden church of British times.(14) The churches both of Wells and Glastonbury must have been built in the old Romanesque style of England which prevailed before the great improvements of Norman Romanesque were brought in in the eleventh century. You must conceive this old church of Saint Andrew as very much smaller, lower, and plainer than the church which we now have, with massive round arches and small round-headed windows, but with one or more tall, slender, unbuttressed towers, imitating the bell-towers of Italy. I do not think that we have a single tower of this kind in Somersetshire, but in other parts of England there are a good many. There is a noble one at Earls Barton in Northamptonshire, and more than one in the city of Lincoln.

Of the foundation attached to the church at this time there is but little to say. The clergy of the cathedral did not as yet form a corporation distinct from the Bishop, and the elaborate system of officers which still exists had not yet begun. The number of canons was probably not fixed; in the next century we incidentally hear that there were only four or five. They had no common buildings besides the church, and they lived no doubt each man in his own house.(15) The revenues of the church seem not to have been large. The ceremony which happened among us last week may make some of you ask whether the canons of Saint Andrew had already

the right of electing the Bishop. This is a question
which it would be hard to answer. I am not prepared with any detailed account of the appointment
of a Bishop of this particular see in the tenth or
eleventh century. But it is certain that the way of
appointing Bishops in those days was very uncertain.(16) It is clear that no Bishop could be consecrated without the King's consent, and that it was
by a document under the King's writ and signature
that the Bishoprick was formally conferred. But the
actual choice of the Bishop seems to have been
made in several ways. Sometimes we hear of the
monks or canons choosing whom they would, and
then going to the King and his Witan or Wise Men,
the great assembly of the nation, to ask for the confirmation of their choice. This confirmation was sometimes given and sometimes refused. Sometimes we
expressly read that the King gave the monks or
canons leave to elect freely. This is exactly what
would happen now, if the *letter missive* should be
lost on the road and the *congé d'élire* should come
by itself.(17) At other times we read of the King
alone, or the King and his Witan, appointing, seemingly without any reference to the monks or canons.
The truth is that in those days the Church and the
nation were more truly two aspects of the same
body than they have ever been since, and that those
questions as to the exact limits of the civil and
ecclesiastical powers, which have gone on, in one
shape or another, from the days of William Rufus till
now, had not yet arisen.

Things thus went on in our church of Wells without

anything very memorable happening, from the days of
Æthelhelm the first Bishop, who was appointed in
909, to those of Duduc, who was Bishop from 1033 to
1060.(¹⁸) Tombs bearing the names of several Bishops
of those days are still to be seen in the church. But
they are all work of the thirteenth century, and, if
the names given to them are trustworthy, Bishop
Jocelin, when he rebuilt the church, must have made
new tombs for his predecessors, a thing which sometimes was done. But when we get to Duduc, we are
getting towards things which ought to be remembered ;
we are getting to the actual local history of the church
of Wells itself, which hitherto it has been hard to
distinguish from the general history of the Church in
England. Duduc was the first Bishop who was not
an Englishman ; he was a Saxon. Of course there
was a sense in which the Bishops before him might
be called Saxons, that is West-Saxons, subjects of
the King of the West-Saxons and probably in most
cases themselves of West-Saxon blood. But Duduc
was a Saxon from the Old-Saxon land in Germany,
the old land of our fathers, and this is always the
meaning of the word Saxon in the history of those
times.(¹⁹) This Bishop Duduc was in high favour both
with King Cnut and afterwards with Eadward the
Confessor. And his name at once brings us to a
story which connects our church of Wells with the
greatest Englishman of those days, though in a way
which has brought undeserved obloquy on his name.
I dare say some of you have read the tale of Harold's
plundering the church of Wells, banishing the Bishop,
bringing the Canons to beggary, and what not. How-

ever, I will read you the story as it stands in Collinson's "History of Somersetshire." He is speaking of the next Bishop Gisa, of whom I shall say more presently.

"On his entry into his diocese, he found the estates of the church in a sad condition; for Harold earl of Wessex, having with his father, Godwin earl of Kent, been banished the kingdom, and deprived of all his estates in this county by King Edward, *who bestowed them on the church of Wells,* had in a piratical manner made a descent in these parts, raised contributions among his former tenants, spoiled the church of all its ornaments, driven away the canons, invaded their possessions, and converted them to his own use. Bishop Giso in vain expostulated with the King on this outrageous usage; but received from the Queen, who was Harold's sister, the manors of Mark and Mudgley, as a trifling compensation for the injuries which his bishoprick had sustained. Shortly after [after 1060] *Harold was restored to King Edward's favour, and made his captain-general;* upon which he in his turn *procured the banishment of Giso,* and when he came to the crown, resumed most of those estates of which he had been deprived. *Bishop Giso continued in banishment till the death of Harold,* and the advancement of the Conqueror to the throne, who in the second year of his reign restored all Harold's estates to the church of Wells, except some small parcels which had been conveyed to the monastery of Gloucester; in lieu of which he gave the manor and advowson of Yatton, and the manor of Winsham." ("History of Somersetshire," iii. 378.)

Now all this, as is commonly the case with what we read in county histories and books of that class, is pure fiction, but it is very curious and instructive to see how the fiction arose. We can trace every step. Collinson improved on the account in Bishop Godwin's Catalogue of Bishops, which was written in the time of Elizabeth.([20]) Godwin improved on the Latin history of Wells, written by a Canon of Wells in the fifteenth century, which is one of our chief authorities on all local matters.([21]) The Canon of Wells, in his turn, improved on the original account given by Bishop Gisa, the person concerned. We have no account from Harold's side, but we have the contemporary version from the other side, and it certainly differs not a little from the version given by our worthy local antiquary. All about Harold's estates being granted to the church of Wells, all about his seizing the estates of the church, all about Gisa being banished and the Canons being driven away, is all pure invention, which has gradually grown up between Gisa's time and Collinson's. Gisa's own account, which is printed in Hunter's Ecclesiastical Documents, is to this effect.([22]) King Cnut had given to Duduc the two lordships of Banwell and Congresbury, not as a possession of his see, but as a private estate. These lands, together with some ornaments and relics, Duduc wished to leave to the see. But on his death Harold, the Earl of the district, took possession of them. This is the whole of the charge. Gisa does not accuse Harold of taking anything which had ever belonged to the see, but only of hindering Duduc's will in favour of the see from taking effect. We thus have Gisa's charge, but we have not Harold's answer. That answer, I conceive, would have been that, as Duduc was a foreigner dying without heirs, he had no power of making a will, but that his property went to the King or to the Earl as his representative. I cannot say for certain whether this would have been good law everywhere, but it certainly would have been good law in some places, and it at once suggests an intelligible explanation of Harold's conduct. But churchmen in those days always held that the Church was always to gain and never to lose, and we find other cases in which laymen who prosecuted legal claims against ecclesiastical bodies are called nearly as hard names as if they had robbed the Church by fraud or violence.([23]) Gisa does not say that he complained to the King or attempted any legal prosecution of the matter; but he made private appeals to Harold and threatened him with excommunication. You must remember that all this concerns only the moveable goods and the lands at Banwell and Congresbury, which, before Duduc's death, had never belonged either to Harold or to the church of Wells. With Winesham Harold had nothing to do; that lordship, Gisa says, was wrongly detained from the see by a man named Ælfsige. Gisa was never banished, and it so happens that the only writ of Harold's which we have is one addressed to Gisa, assuring him of his friendship and confirming him and his see in all their possessions.([24]) Gisa himself adds that Harold, after his election to the Crown, promised to restore the two lordships and to make other gifts as well. This he was hindered from doing by what

Gisa calls God's judgement upon him, that is to say, by the Conquest of England.([25])

Now this is a very remarkable story, as showing how tales grow, like snowballs rolled along the ground, and how dangerous it is to take things on trust from late and careless writers. You see at once how utterly different Gisa's own account of his own doings is from that in Collinson. The Canon of Wells and Bishop Godwin give the story in intermediate forms. I should strongly recommend those who are able to get at the books to compare all four accounts together. There cannot be a better example of the growth of a legend.

This Bishop Gisa, who succeeded Duduc in the year 1060, was a remarkable man in our local history. Like Duduc, he was a foreigner. Like several other Bishops at that time, he came from Lotharingia or Lorraine. But you must remember that the name Lorraine then meant, not only Upper Lorraine which is now part of France, but Lower Lorraine, a great part of which is now part of the Kingdom of Belgium. Gisa in short was what we should now call a Belgian, and he probably spoke the old tongue of those parts, which is one of the tongues of the Continent which is most like our own. He complains that, when he came to his diocese, he found his church mean and its revenues small; so much so that the four or five canons who were there had to beg their bread.([26]) Of course I need not say that this is an exaggerated way of talking; but we may well believe that, like many a poor clergyman still, they were glad of any help that well-disposed people would give them. It is worth notice that another Bishop of the same time and of the same nation, Hermann, Bishop of the Wilsætas, complained that the revenues of his church at Ramsbury were so small that they could not maintain any monks or canons at all. Hermann mended matters in one way by getting the Bishoprick of Dorsetshire or Sherborne joined to that of Wiltshire and Berkshire, and in the end he moved his see to Salisbury, that is of course Old Sarum, whence it was afterwards again moved to the new city of that name.([27]) Gisa set to work to increase the revenues of his church by buying and begging in all directions. King Eadward gave him Wedmore; his wife, the Lady Eadgyth—remember that the proper title of the wife of a West-Saxon King was not Queen but Lady—gave him Mark and Mudgeley; William the Conqueror gave him the disputed lordships of Banwell and Winesham, and he bought Combe and lands at Litton and Wormestor or Worminster.([28]) He was thus able to make a good provision for his canons; you will doubtless remember that many of the places which I have just spoken of give their names to prebends in the church of Wells to this day. He also greatly increased the number of canons, but he did something more. Among the things which he complains of is that the canons of Wells before his time had no cloister or refectory. This means that they did not live in common, but lived, after the manner of English secular priests, each man in his own house. They therefore had no need of a common refectory or dining-hall, nor had they any need of a cloister. In a monastery the cloister is one of the most important parts of the building; it is the centre of everything, all the other parts gathering round it; and it is always built in one particular place and of one particular shape, namely a square north or south of the nave of the church. In a monastery in short the cloister is a necessity; in a secular church it is a luxury, a thing which may be very well left alone. In our secular churches therefore we sometimes find a cloister and sometimes not, and, when there was one, it might be built of any shape and in any position that might be thought good. But in Gisa's country of Lorraine the secular canons were used to live in a much stricter way than they did in England. They were not monks, because they did not take vows; but they lived much more after the manner of monks, dwelling together with a common refectory and a common dormitory or sleeping-room, and being governed by very strict rules which had been drawn up by Chrodegang, Bishop of Metz in Upper Lorraine.([29]) You will see that the main object of all this was to hinder them from marrying, which the English secular priests, living each man in his own house, often did. Gisa's great object was to bring this discipline, the discipline, as he says, of his own country, into his church of Wells. This was what several Bishops about the same time were doing elsewhere. About a hundred years before Adalbero, Archbishop of Rheims, had done the same in his church, the metropolitan church of France.([30]) But Rheims, you may remark, though in France and the head church of France, is quite near enough to the borders of Lorraine to come within the reach of Lotharingian influences. So in our own country, at this very time Leofric Bishop of Exeter was introducing the same discipline into his church.([31]) But we find that Leofric, though by birth an Englishman, or perhaps rather a Welshman of Cornwall, had been brought up in Lorraine. It is always from Lorraine, in one shape or another, that this kind of change seems to come. And we have quite enough to show that Englishmen did not like it, as the changes which were brought in by Gisa and Leofric did not last very long either at Wells or at Exeter. Gisa, however, carried his point for the time. He built a cloister, a refectory, and whatever other buildings were needed for his purpose, and made the Canons live after the Lotharingian fashion. As their chief officer he appointed one Isaac, one of their own body, and whom they themselves chose. He was called the Provost, and his chief business was to look after the temporal concerns of the church.

Now in this account there are many things worthy of careful notice. First, mark the full authority of the Bishop in his own church; Gisa seems to do whatever he pleases. We need not suppose that he did what he did without obtaining the consent of his Chapter in some shape or other; but it is plain that the Bishop was still, to say the least, the chief mover in everything. One is also inclined to think that before Gisa's time the Canons had no property distinct from that of the Bishop. A large portion of his new acquisitions was bestowed to the benefit of the Canons; but it appears from Domesday that what they held at the time of the Survey was all held under the Bishop.([32]) Secondly, mark the very important change which Gisa made in the constitution of the church of Wells by bringing in the Lotharingian discipline. He did not, like some other Prelates, drive out his canons and put monks in their stead, nor yet did he, as was done at some other places, compel his canons to take monastic vows. The Canons of Wells, after his changes, still remained secular priests and not regulars. But the changes which he made were all in a monastic direction. They brought in something of the strictness of monastic discipline among a body of men who had hitherto lived in a very much freer way. I cannot help thinking that the rule of Chrodegang was but the small end of the wedge, and that before long it would, if not by Gisa, by some reforming Bishop or other, have been developed into the rule of Saint Benedict. But the next Bishop was not a reforming Bishop, and the fear of the Canons of Wells being displaced to make room for monks, or being themselves turned into monks, happily passed away. Gisa, there can be no doubt, was a good man and a diligent and conscientious Bishop, though some of his doings were such as we Englishmen are not likely to approve. At last, after being Bishop twenty-eight years, he died in 1088, and was buried under an arch in the wall on the north side of the high altar, as his predecessor Duduc was on the south side.([33]) This notice is important; it shows that Gisa, among all his works of other kinds, did not rebuild the church itself; it also shows, by speaking of an arch in the wall, that the eastern part of the church had no aisles.

The next Bishop was quite another kind of man.

I know not whether he is reverenced at Bath, but we at Wells have certainly no reason to love his memory. You will remember that, as Gisa was Bishop from 1060 to 1088, the Norman Conquest of England came in his time. One result of that event was that all the Bishopricks and Abbeys of England were gradually filled by strangers, and much greater strangers to England than Duduc and Gisa had been. The new Bishops and Abbots, just as much as the new Earls, were almost all Normans or Frenchmen, who, I suspect, seldom learned to talk English. The first Bishop of Somersetshire after the Conquest was John de Villulâ, a Frenchman from Tours, who was appointed by William Rufus. About this time there was a great movement, which had begun under Edward the Confessor and which went on under William the Conqueror, for moving the sees or *bishopstools* of Bishops from smaller towns to greater ones. Thus, in our own part of England, Bishop Leofric, in King Edward's time, removed the united see of Devonshire and Cornwall from Crediton to Exeter, and in King William's time Bishop Hermann removed the united see of Dorsetshire and Wiltshire from Ramsbury and Sherborne to Salisbury. By Salisbury you will of course remember that I mean Old Sarum and not New. The historian William of Malmesbury, who wrote under Henry the First, calls this change the removal of Bishopricks from villages or small towns to cities. And among the villages or small towns from which Bishopricks were removed I am sorry to say that he reckons our city of Wells.([34]) For the first thing that the new Bishop John did

was to remove his bishopstool from the church of
Saint Andrew at Wells to the church of Saint Peter at
Bath, on which William of Malmesbury remarks that
Andrew, although the elder brother, was obliged to
give way to his younger brother Simon.(35) Bath was
then, as now, a much larger town than Wells, and was
a walled city, which Wells never has been. It was
an old Roman town, which had been taken by the
West-Saxons in 577, a good while before Somersetshire
south of the Axe became English.(36) The church
of Saint Peter there was founded by Offa, King of the
Mercians, for secular canons, but King Eadgar had, as
in so many other churches, put monks instead, and
Bath had ever since been a famous monastery. So, if
the Bishop's see is necessarily to be fixed in the
greatest town in the diocese, Bath was undoubtedly
the right place, but it had the disadvantage of being
much less central than Wells, being, as we all know,
quite in a corner of the diocese. The Abbey of Bath
was just then vacant by the death of the Abbot
Ælfsige, an Englishman who had contrived to keep his
office all through the reign of William the Conqueror;
so Bishop John persuaded King William Rufus to grant
the Abbey of Bath for the increase of the Bishoprick of
Somersetshire.(37) This was done by a charter in 1088,
which was confirmed by two charters of Henry the
First in 1100 and 1111. In the next year the Bishop
begged or bought of the King the whole town of Bath,
which had lately been burned. The effect of these
changes was that the Abbey of Bath was merged in
the Bishoprick. There was no longer a separate
Abbot, but the Bishop was Abbot; the church of

Saint Peter became his cathedral church, and its Prior and monks became his Chapter. The Bishop also, by his grant or purchase from the King, became temporal lord of the town. Bishop John, having thus got possession of Bath and all that was in it, spiritual and temporal, reigned there at first somewhat sternly. He was, as I have said, a foreigner; he was also a skilful physician and fond of learned men of every kind. The monks of Bath, no doubt mostly Englishmen, he despised as ignorant barbarians; so he oppressed them and cut their living very short, till afterwards, we are told, he repented, and gave them their possessions back again.(38) He also rebuilt the church of Bath, now become his cathedral church, and greatly enriched it with ornaments and the like, and then, after being Bishop for thirty-six years, he died and was buried in 1124.

But it more concerns us to know what was going on at Wells all this time. The see had been altogether taken away, so much so that one of the charters of Henry the First speaks of the see of all Somersetshire having been moved to Bath from the town which is called Wells. I conceive that the Bishop of Bath now looked on Wells simply as one of the lordships of the see, just like Banwell, Evercreech, Wookey, or any other, where the Bishops had houses and where they occasionally lived. So, among his other doings, Bishop John built himself a house at Wells. But the way in which he found himself a site and materials was a somewhat remarkable one. For it was by pulling down all the buildings that Gisa had built for the use of the Canons, and building his own house on the spot.(39) Now this shows that either the church or the Bishop's Palace has changed its place since the time of John of Tours. For we may be sure that Gisa built his cloister, refectory, and dormitory close to the church, just as they would be in a monastery. Therefore, if John built his house on their site, it must have been much nearer to the church than the present palace is. Nothing is left of either the church or the palace as they stood then, and it is most likely that the site of the palace has been changed, and that Gisa's canonical buildings and John's manor-house both stood where the cloister, library, &c. stand now. But I thought it worth while to mention this, because it was not very uncommon, when a church was rebuilt, to build the new church a little way off from the old one.(40) The reason for this was, that the service might go on in the old church while the new one was building; and when the new church was finished, the old one was pulled down and the new used instead. It is therefore quite possible that our present cathedral does not stand quite on the same site as the church which was standing in Gisa and John's time. But on the whole the chances are the other way.

The Canons of Wells were thus turned out of the buildings which Gisa had made for them, and were driven to live where they could in the town.(41) The great and learned Bishop of Bath cared nothing about them, or rather he made spoil of them in every way. A portion of their estates, valued then at thirty pounds a year, was held by the Bishop's steward, Hildebert by name, who seems also to have been his brother and to have held the office of Provost of the Canons. On

Hildebert's death, the estate, by the Bishop's assent, passed as an hereditary possession to his son John, who is described as Archdeacon and Provost.([42]) As I understand the matter, the estate became a kind of impropriation; Hildebert, John, and their heirs held the estate, and paid the Canons a fixed rent-charge. For though we read of the estate being taken away from the Church, yet we also read incidentally that Provost John paid each Canon sixty shillings yearly.([43]) This would seem to show that there were ten Canons, among whom the thirty pounds had to be divided. But as we read that, when Bishop Robert recovered the property, he paid each Canon a hundred shillings, it would seem that the estate increased in value, but that John simply paid the Canons their old stipends, taking to himself the surplus, which should no doubt have been employed either in raising the stipends of the existing Canons or else in increasing their number. This is the kind of abuse which we constantly light upon in all manner of institutions, and we see that at all events it is not a new abuse. Canons in their own infancy were treated by Provosts much as Canons, in the days of their greater developement, have in different places treated Minor Canons, Singing Men, Grammar-Boys, and Poor Knights. The peculiar thing is that the Provostship became hereditary, subject only to this fixed charge, exactly like a lay rectory charged with a payment to the Vicar.

I think then that, however our Bath neighbours may look at him, we at Wells have a right to set down Bishop John of Tours as the worst enemy that our church had from the eighth century to the sixteenth.

We are told that he repented, but it must have been an ineffectual kind of repentance, as he made no restitution.(44) Or we may say that his repentance was geographical, for a deed is extant in which he restores to the monks of Bath all that he had taken from them, but there is no sign that he restored anything to the Canons of Wells.(45) Still his doings had one effect; the Lotharingian discipline was broken up for ever, and the secular priests of Wells were never again constrained to sleep in a common dormitory or to dine in a common refectory. John thus indirectly helped to put things on the footing which they assumed under the next Bishop but one, and which, in its main features, has been retained to this day. It is that Bishop, Robert by name, whose episcopate forms the natural boundary of the first portion of my subject. Hitherto I have had to deal with a church and a Chapter of Wells; but hardly with the church and Chapter which at present exist. I have had to speak of the early beginning of things, of fabrics and institutions alike which were far from having reached their full developement. With Robert a new era begins alike in architectural, capitular, and municipal matters. He was a founder in every sense. He rebuilt the fabrics of both his churches. He settled the relations between those two churches as they remained till the suppression of the monastery of Bath in the sixteenth century. He gave the Chapter of Wells a new constitution, which, with some changes in detail, it still retains. Last, but not least, he gave the first charter of incorporation to the burghers who had gradually come to dwell under the shadow of the minster. He may therefore be looked upon as the founder of Wells, church and city alike, as they now stand. The reign of this memorable Prelate therefore marks the first stage in my story; I will therefore now bring my first lecture to an end, and will reserve a detailed account of the important episcopate of Robert to form the beginning of my account of the mediæval, as distinguished from the early, history of the church of Wells.

LECTURE II.

IN my former Lecture I did my best to trace the history of the church of Wells from the earliest days. We have seen its small beginnings, a colony of priests planted in a newly-conquered land, with their home fixed on a small oasis between the wild hill-country on the one side and the never-ending fen on the other. There their church had risen, and settlers had gathered round it; it had grown into the seat of a Bishop, the spiritual centre of the surrounding country, a rival in fame and reverence of that great island church which stood as a memorial of the past days of the conquered, while Wells rose as a witness of the presence of the conquerors. We have seen one Prelate of foreign birth at once vastly increase the power and revenues of his see and try to subject his clergy to the yoke of a foreign rule against which the instincts of Englishmen revolted. We have seen another foreigner undo the work of his predecessor alike for good and for evil; we have seen him forsake church and city altogether, and remove his episcopal chair to a statelier and safer dwelling-place. We have seen the local foundation again brought back to a state lower than the poor and feeble condition out of which Gisa had raised it. We now come to the great benefactor whom we may fairly look upon as the founder of Wells as it is, the man who put the

Bishoprick and Chapter into the shape with which we are all familiar, and who moreover gave to the city its first municipal being.

On this last head I shall not enlarge. The subject is so completely the property of others both present and absent that I should feel myself the merest intruder if I attempted to dwell upon it. I will rather go on with those parts of Bishop Robert's career which more directly concern my subject, and look at him in three lights, as his actions concern respectively the Bishoprick, the Chapter, and the fabric of the church.

After the death of John of Tours the see was held by one Godfrey, a countryman of Gisa's from Lower Lorraine, and therefore somewhat nearer to an Englishman than a mere Frenchman like John. His promotion was owing to his being a chaplain of the Queen, Henry the First's second wife, Adeliza of Löwen, with whom he had doubtless come into England.([1]) He is described as being of noble birth, mild, and pious, but perhaps mere mildness was not the virtue which was most needed in those days. All that we hear of him is that he tried to get back the Canons' lands from John the Archdeacon, but that King Henry and Roger Bishop of Salisbury, who was a mighty man in those days, hindered him. He died in 1135. Then came Robert. He was a rare case of a Bishoprick in those times being held by a man who could be called in any sense an Englishman. As a rule, the great ecclesiastical offices were now given to men who were not only not of Old-English descent, but who were not even the sons of Normans or other strangers settled in England. Utter foreigners, men born on the Continent, were commonly preferred to either. But Robert was a Fleming by descent and born in England. As a native of the land, and sprung from one of those foreign nations whose blood and speech is most closely akin to our own, we may welcome him a countryman, in days when the most part of the land was parcelled out among men who did not even speak our tongue. He had been a monk at Lewes at Sussex, and was promoted by the favour of Henry of Blois, Bishop of Winchester, the famous brother of King Stephen. Henry had been Abbot of Glastonbury before he became Bishop, and, what is more, he kept the Abbey along with his Bishoprick. He is said to have sent for Robert to look after the affairs of the monastery; that is, I suppose, to act as his deputy after he became Bishop.(²) Thus we see that the comfortable practice of pluralities, and what somebody calls the "sacred principle of delegation,"—that is to say, the holding two or more incompatible offices and leaving their duties to be done by others or not to be done at all,—are inventions in which the nineteenth century was forestalled by the twelfth. Robert next from deputy Abbot of Glastonbury became Bishop of Bath, and he seems to have set himself manfully to work to bring his diocese and its two head churches out of the state of confusion into which the changes of John of Tours had brought them. First of all with regard to the Bishoprick. You understand of course that the removal of the see from Wells to Bath had been made without the consent of the Canons of Wells, who had an undoubted right to be consulted about the matter. In ecclesiastical theory a Bishop and his Chapter are very much like a King and his Parliament; neither of them can do any important act without the consent of the other. And here a thing had been done for which of all others the consent of the Wells Chapter ought to have been had, as their most precious rights had been taken away from them. All this time they had never formally submitted to the change, and they had been always complaining of the wrongful removal of the see, and asserting their own rights against the usurpations of the monks of Bath. And it is to be noticed that the change had never been approved or recognized by any Pope. The Bishops of Somersetshire were still known in official language at Rome as *Episcopi Fontanenses* or Bishops of Wells, not as *Episcopi Bathonienses* or Bishops of Bath. Robert now procured that the episcopal position of Bath should be recognized, and from this time for some while after our Bishops are commonly called Bishops of Bath.([3]) But it would seem that this is merely a contracted form, for the style of Bishop of Bath and Wells, with which we are all so familiar, is found before very long. And there can be no doubt that the controversy was now settled by Robert on these terms, that Bath should take precedence of Wells, but that the Bishop should have his throne in both churches, that he should be chosen by the monks of Bath and the Canons of Wells conjointly, or by deputies appointed by the two Chapters, and that those episcopal acts which needed the confirmation of the Chapter should be confirmed both by the Convent of Bath and by the Chapter of Wells.(⁴) There are deeds hanging up in this very room to which you will see the confirmation of both those bodies. The Bishop of Somersetshire thus had two cathedral churches, as was also the case with the Bishop of Coventry and Lichfield, and as has been the case with the Bishop of Gloucester and Bristol since those sees were joined within our own memory. This arrangement lasted till the cathedral church of Bath was suppressed under Henry the Eighth, after which, by an Act of Parliament passed in 1542, the Chapter of Wells was made the sole Chapter for the Bishop.(⁵) Things thus came back, as far as Wells was concerned, to much the same state as they had been in before the changes of John of Tours, except that Bath still forms a part of the Bishop's style. But since the Act of Henry the Eighth it has been a mere title, as the Bishop is Bishop of Bath in no sense except that in which he is Bishop of Taunton or of any other place in the diocese. He is elected by the Chapter of Wells only; he is enthroned in the church of Wells only; and when Saint Peter's church at Bath was set up again in the reign of James the First, it was not as a cathedral, but as a simple parish church.

Bishop Robert, having thus settled himself as Bishop of Bath *and* Wells, with two churches under his special care, began to set to work to put in order whatever needed reform in both of them. He enlarged and finished the church of Bath, if he did not actually rebuild it from the ground. I speak thus doubtingly, because our accounts do not exactly agree.

The little book called "Historiola de Primordiis Episcopatûs Somersetensis" says that "he himself caused the church of the Blessed Peter the Apostle at Bath to be built at a great cost."[6] But the history commonly quoted as the Canon of Wells says only that "he finished the fabric of the church of Bath which had been begun by John of Tours."[7] Now the "Historiola" is the earlier authority, and that which we should generally believe rather than the other, whenever there is any difference between the two. But, on the other hand, stories generally grow greater and not smaller; a man's exploits are much more likely to be made too much of by those who repeat the tale than to be made too little of. When therefore the later writer attributes to Robert less than the earlier one does, one is tempted to think that the earlier writer exaggerated or spoke in a loose way, and that the Canon of Wells had some good reason for his correction. And this is the more to be noticed, because we shall find exactly the same difference when we come to the accounts which the two writers give of what Robert did at Wells. It is indeed said that the church and city of Bath were again destroyed by fire in 1135, and that this made Robert's rebuilding necessary. But the phrase of being destroyed by fire is often used very laxly of cases where a building, like York Minster within the memory of some people, was simply a good deal damaged, and had to be repaired, but did not need to be wholly rebuilt. At any rate, whether Robert altogether rebuilt or only finished, the great church of Saint Peter at Bath was now brought to perfection. Do not for a moment think that this is the Abbey Church of Bath which is now standing, and which I do not doubt that a great many of you know very well. The church of John and Robert was of course built in the Romanesque style with round arches, and in that particular variety of Romanesque which had been imported by Eadward the Confessor from Normandy into England, and which we therefore call the Norman style. But the present church of Bath is one of the latest examples of our latest English Gothic, and of that special variety of it which forms the local Perpendicular style of Somersetshire. Moreover the Romanesque church was very much larger than the present one, which covers the site of its nave only. One little bit of the Romanesque building, the arch between the south aisle and the south transept, is still to be seen at the present east end. The fact is that the later Bishops of Bath and Wells were not at all of the same mind as John of Tours. They lived much more at Wells than at Bath, and took much more care of the church of Wells. Bath indeed was quite neglected, and by the end of the fifteenth century the church was in a great state of decay. It was then, in the year 1500, that Bishop Oliver King and Prior Bird began to build the present church on a smaller scale and in a widely different style of architecture. Besides what he did to the church, Bishop Robert built or rebuilt all the conventual buildings of his Abbey of Bath, the cloister, refectory, dormitory, and the rest, all which were necessary for the monks of Bath, though the secular priests of Wells could do without them.([8])

It is to be noticed that Bishop Robert, himself a monk, when he began to reconstitute the Church of Wells in the way of which I now have to speak, made no attempt to bring in monks instead of secular canons, or even to subject the Canons to the same half-monastic discipline which had been brought in by Gisa. All his changes in fact tended in an exactly opposite direction. Hitherto the Canons had been altogether dependent on the Bishop. They do not seem to have formed a distinct corporation, and the lands which they held, when they were not taken away from them altogether were held by them as the Bishop's tenants. All Robert's changes tended to give them greater distinctness and independence. The first business was to get back the lands which had been alienated by the connivance of Bishop John, and which Bishop Godfrey had in vain tried to get back. John the Archdeacon, we are told, repented on his death-bed, and straitly charged his brother Reginald to restore the lands. This he now did; he came to Bath and surrendered everything to the Bishop, but we shall presently see that his vested interest was thought worthy of some respect. It is now that we are told that, instead of the sixty shillings which John had paid each Canon yearly, the Bishop was able to pay them a hundred shillings.(⁹) And now, to hinder anything of the kind happening again, Robert put the constitution and revenues of his Chapter on altogether a new footing. The Canons became a separate corporation, distinct from the Bishop; and, besides this, each Canon became for some purposes a separate corporation sole, distinct alike from the

Bishop and from his brother Canons. For Robert first founded the dignities and prebends of the Church of Wells. The dignities are the chief offices of the Chapter, those of the Dean, the Precentor, the Chancellor, the Treasurer, and the Sub-Dean, all which offices still remain, to which we may add the Provostship, which still went on, and the Subchantership; these two no longer exist. Of these the Deanery and the Precentorship were certainly founded by Robert. Of the others I do not feel quite certain whether they were founded by Robert or by Jocelin.([10]) But in any case all that Jocelin did in this matter was to carry out the plans of Robert somewhat more fully, and we may fairly discuss the whole constitution as one work at this point. We need not suppose that all these offices were absolutely new; for instance, there must always have been a Precentor, or some one discharging the Precentor's duties in the immediate government of the choir. But at all events these offices were not till now distinct and permanent foundations, with a special *status* and distinct revenues of their own, which they now became. In the Dean especially the Canons now got for the first time a head of their own body distinct from the Bishop. Now as to the prebends. There is a corrupt way of speaking in use now of calling some few members of the Chapter *Canons*, as if the name belonged to them only, and calling the rest of the body *Prebendaries*, as if they were something different and, I suppose, something inferior. That this is a mere corruption is well known to every one who knows anything of the history of these foundations. But it is also made very plain by the language of official documents to this day. Whenever a new Prebendary is installed, he is still installed into "the Canonry or Prebend" of so and so; and when the whole Chapter is summoned for the election of a Bishop, all its members without distinction are still summoned by the title of Canons. The truth is that every member of the cathedral body is at once a Canon and a Prebendary. Canon and Prebendary are two different names for the same man looked at in two different characters. He is a Canon as one of the capitular body, a member of the corporation called the Dean and Chapter; he is also a Prebendary as holding—or of later years not holding—a certain prebend, *præbenda*, or separate estate, in regard to which he himself forms a corporation sole. The priests of Saint Andrew's had been Canons all along, but they first became Prebendaries under Bishop Robert. For it was he who first founded the prebends or separate estates. He divided the property of the Canons into two parts. Certain estates were to be held by the whole body in common as a corporation aggregate. Certain other estates were cut up into smaller portions or *prebends*, of which each Canon held one as a corporation sole. Such and such lands or tithes were attached as a prebend to the Deanery, to the Precentorship, and so on through the whole body; those Canons who did not hold any dignity, such as Dean or Precentor, being called Prebendaries of the place where their estates or *corpses* lay, Wormestor, Buckland, or any other. Some estates, as those of Combe and Wedmore, were so large as to form several prebends; thus we get the titles which sound so odd, Wedmore the first, Combe the twelfth, and the like. Thus each Canon came to have as it were two beings. As a Canon, he was one of a body, enjoying rights and discharging duties in common with his brethren. As a Prebendary he was independent, holding his own prebendal estate like any other holder of a benefice. But mark that the title of Canon, a title of office and duty, is clearly a more honourable title than that of Prebendary, which is a mere title of property. And mark again that, now that all the prebendal estates are transferred to the Ecclesiastical Commissioners, it may fairly be doubted whether there are any Prebendaries left, save the few who were appointed before those changes began. But there is nothing in the Act of Parliament which brought about those changes which at all touches the *status* of a non-residentiary Canon in any point except that of his property. What I want you to bear in mind is that, when a non-residentiary Canon becomes a Residentiary, he is not, as people commonly talk, changed from a Prebendary into a Canon. He was a Canon before, and, saving my own objection which I have just started, he remains a Prebendary afterwards. How the distinction between residentiary and non-residentiary Canons came about I shall explain presently.

The Church of Wells thus received a new constitution at the hands of Bishop Robert, who was helped in his undertaking by King Stephen and by his former patron, the King's brother Henry, Bishop of Winchester.([11]) This constitution is essentially the same as that which, in theory at least, exists still, and it is one which, in all its main features, is shared by Wells with all the other cathedral churches of the Old Foundation. The cathedral churches of the Old Foundation are those which have always had secular canons, which therefore were not suppressed at the dissolution of monasteries, but have gone on uninterruptedly with essentially the same constitution down to our own time. Such, besides our own church, are the neighbouring churches of Salisbury and Exeter. Such, in other parts of England, are York, London, Lincoln, Lichfield, Hereford, Chichester, and the four cathedrals of Wales. The churches of the New Foundation are those which in the time of Henry the Eighth were served by monks, which were therefore dissolved along with the other monasteries, and all of which, except Bath and Coventry, were refounded by him as Chapters of secular canons. Such was our old mother church of Winchester; such was the common mother church at Canterbury; such were Rochester, Norwich, Worcester, Durham, and the newer sees of Ely and Carlisle. With these are also reckoned the churches which became cathedral by Henry planting Bishops in them for the first time, Oxford, Peterborough, Saint Werburgh's at Chester, our own neighbours of Gloucester and Bristol, and Westminster, which lost its Bishop in the next reign, and is now only a collegiate church. And to these I suppose we must again add the churches of Ripon and Manchester, which have become cathedral in our own time. In all these the constitution is very different from that of the churches of the Old Foundation; among other things, they have not that variety of officers, each with his separate duties and revenues, which are to be found in the Old Foundations. And the influence of the Crown is much greater in the New Foundations than in the Old. Their Deans have always been appointed by the Crown, and in several of them the Canons also are appointed either by the Crown or by the Lord Chancellor. In the Old Foundations the Dignitaries and other Canons, except the Dean, have always been appointed by the Bishop. In the Welsh churches the Deans also have always been, and still are, appointed by the Bishops.([12]) In the others the Canons elected their own Dean, but a custom gradually came in by which the Crown recommended a person, who was always chosen. But within the reign of the present Queen, there chanced to be some legal objection to the person recommended by the Crown to the Chapter of Exeter, so that the Canons freely elected their own Dean, who held his place till his death; only meanwhile an Act of Parliament was passed, vesting in the Crown the appointment to the Old Deaneries as well as to the New. You will see easily that, though the connexion between the Bishop and his Chapter is everywhere much weakened from what it once was and from what it ought to be, it still is much closer in the churches of the Old Foundation than in those of the New.

It is to the wise and careful gradation of officers, each with his special function, in our own church and in the other churches of the Old Foundation, that I wish specially to call your attention. I assume of course that all are constantly resident, as constantly resident as a parish clergyman is on his living. I assume of course that none of them holds any preferment besides his cathedral office. These two conditions are necessary to the effective carrying out of the ancient scheme ; it is owing to the breach of them, a breach which is no new thing, but which began almost from the beginning, that a most wisely and beautifully ordered system has gradually become a mere name. When offices whose duties require the constant presence of their holders on the spot are held by men who are resident for three months only or not resident at all ; when there is not even any provision for the proper discharge of their duties by deputy, the whole scheme of those offices fails, and their mere empty titles become mockeries. The great offices of the cathedral, those of Dean, Precentor, Chancellor, and Treasurer, are sinecures in the legal sense, as being without cure of souls ;([13]) but they were certainly not meant to be sinecures in any other sense. They are offices any one of which would afford ample occupation for a studious and thoughtful man, whose soul was in his work and who loved the institution of which he was a member. The Dean is the President of the Chapter, the general superintendent of the whole institution. I can say from the examples of men alike dead and living, that when that important post is held by a man who understands its duties, it is anything but a sinecure, anything but useless. A man of ability and zeal, to whom the cathedral and everything about it supplies some labour of love at every step, who knows and loves every stone of the fabric, whose heart answers to every note of its services, to whom every tittle of its history is a living thing, will not find the office of a Dean an idle or an irksome one. Unencumbered by any parochial charge, he will influence men's minds as the chief preacher of the cathedral church, and as continuing the old missionary functions of capitular bodies by preaching on fitting occasions in other parts of the diocese. As the chief presbyter of the city and diocese, he will be foremost in every good work within that city and diocese, ever at his post, keeping up order and discipline alike by precept and by example, dispensing the simple but liberal hospitality enjoined by ecclesiastical rule. As the President of the Bishop's Council, he will be the Bishop's right-hand man in his presence, and his most natural representative in his absence. Such I conceive to have been the sort of Dean whom good Bishop Robert wished to see at the head of his Chapter; such Deans there have been and still are, and under such Deans cathedral institutions are not found to be useless. Hardly less important are the functions of the officer second in rank, the Precentor. To his lot falls the immediate management of the cathedral services; he is, as Bishop Godwin says, "the Precentor to govern the choir."[14] Here is work, full and worthy work, for an accomplished musician and profound liturgical scholar. It is plain that the duties of both these great officers are constant, that the presence of some one to discharge those duties is always needed. The pious care either of Robert or of Jocelin therefore provided for their occasional and unavoidable absence, by the foundation of two officers, holding the rank of dignitaries, whose duty it was to supply their place on such occasions, namely, the Sub-Dean and the Sub-Chanter. The office of Sub-Chanter no longer exists; the Sub-Dean, I need not say, is still among us. Next comes the Chancellor, the Chancellor of the Church, whom I hope no one will confound with the Chancellor of the Diocese, a judicial functionary with whom my history has nothing to do. His business, says Godwin, is "to instruct the younger sort of Canons." But his business is more than this: he is the great educational officer of the church and diocese; the head and centre of all that is done in that way in the city and diocese. Here, I need not say, is practical work enough for any man, especially in these days. One very natural part of his functions is now very efficiently discharged among us, but it is discharged by other members of the capitular body, and by them hardly in their capitular character.([15]) The last of these great officers is the Treasurer, who must not be taken for a bursar or steward; his duty is to "look to the ornaments of the church." His duties are certainly less wide and less important than those of his brethren: but they are duties which to an ecclesiastical antiquary would be a labour of love; and, if they were combined with the special care of the church itself, with the office of Master of the Fabric, they would rise in importance to a level with any of the others. Such were the dignitaries, each, besides his share of the general revenue, having his own special prebendal estate. Such was the case with the other Canons also, the whole body amounting in Robert's time to about twenty-two. Other

Bishops increased their numbers till they reached the full tale of fifty, at which they still remain.

In what I have just been saying, I have been drawing an ideal picture, a picture of the great officers of a cathedral body, as they ought to be, as I doubt not that their founders meant them to be, but not as I suppose that they ever will be, or that they ever were. But in this, as in all other matters, it is well to make our ideal the highest possible. If we aim at the highest mark, we shall, in this imperfect world, most likely not hit it, but we shall assuredly come much nearer to it than if we are content to aim at a lower mark. What hindered this goodly scheme from being carried out for any length of time, what probably hindered it from being ever in its fulness carried out at all, was the vice of the age, the inveterate tendency to pluralities and non-residence. In fairness to our own age we must say that the instances of those abuses which still remain, even those which remained in the last generation, are trifles compared with the pluralities and non-residence of the Middle Ages. But in fairness to those ages we must also say that the pluralities and non-residence of those days had not always their root in mere unscrupulous greediness, but in a peculiar view of ecclesiastical offices, which we now hold to be wrong, but which the circumstances of those times rendered natural. The true theory of the endowment of an ecclesiastical office doubtless is that an office is instituted for the common good; it is the business of its holder to discharge its duties in person; an endowment is attached to it, not as mere payment for work done, but as a maintenance for its holder and a means of enabling him to discharge his duties efficiently and liberally. But the feudal notions which were then prevalent caused ecclesiastical offices to be looked on in quite another light. Temporal estates, temporal *benefices*—for the word is just as correctly applied to a lay fee as to a bishoprick or a rectory ([16])—were held of the lord by the tenure of performing some service, military or otherwise, for the lord's behoof. So that those services were efficiently performed, it was not necessary, it was not always possible, that the holder of the fief should perform them in his own person. And of course there has been no time when temporal men have had any scruple, nor is there any reason why they should have any scruple, in multiplying their temporal estates as largely as they honestly can. A false analogy led men to look on ecclesiastical offices in the same feudal light. They were looked on as benefices rather than as offices, as estates held by a certain service, by the discharge of certain ecclesiastical duties, but, provided those duties were performed, it was thought to matter little whether the holder of the benefice performed them personally or by deputy. Here and there a specially virtuous man, a saint in short, would not cumber himself with any office whose duties he could not perform in his own person. But men of ordinary virtue, men who were not scrupulous beyond the public opinion of their day, did not hesitate to heap benefice upon benefice, and thought their consciences were perfectly clear if the duties of each were discharged by a competent deputy. It is like any other evil fashion; we admire those who rise above it; we are not hard on those who conform to it, provided they do not sink before the received morality of the time. But the prevalence of this view of ecclesiastical property was enough to undermine from the very beginning all such pious schemes as those of our Bishop Robert. And we find that Robert was himself driven to a course which was probably unavoidable, but which reads very like a compromise, not to say a job. We have seen that Reginald the brother of Archdeacon John restored the capitular estate. But we find that Robert invested Reginald with the office of Precentor, and, what is more, attached to it as its prebend the whole estate of Combe, an estate so valuable that it was provided that on Reginald's death it should be divided into five prebends.([17]) Possibly Reginald did not personally lose much by surrendering the estate of the Canons, when his prebend, like Benjamin's mess, was five times as much as any of theirs. And it is further to be noticed that two nephews of Reginald, two knights called Payne of Pembridge and Roger Witing, did not willingly acquiesce in an arrangement which cut them off from the succession to what they had learned to look on as an hereditary estate. In the reign of Henry the Second they brought an action to recover the lands which had been restored to the Church by their uncle Reginald. It is said in a marked way that this happened after the death of Stephen and the accession of Henry. This looks therefore as if Henry had some ill-feeling against a Bishop who had been so specially favoured by his mother's rival. It sounds very strange to read that, though the claim of the two knights was strongly withstood by the Bishop, by Ivo the first Dean, and by their own uncle Reginald, now Precentor, yet in the end the matter had to be compromised, and the claims of Reginald's nephews were bought off with a payment of twenty marks.([18]) This case is only one of many in which the Church found it very hard to recover lands of which it had once parted with the possession, whether in the usual form of a lease for three lives—a very old custom indeed ([19])—or of any other. We have no statement from the side of Reginald's nephews, and it is quite possible that their case may really have been not unlike that of those who in our own day have enfranchised lands held of ecclesiastical bodies. In any case the name of one of the claimants is worth notice, and local genealogists may perhaps be able to tell me something about his descendants. It would be remarkable indeed if Roger Witing, the obstinate enemy of the Church of Wells, should prove to have been a forefather of Richard Whiting, the Abbot and martyr of Glastonbury.

In the deed by which Bishop Robert founds the Deanery and Precentorship, he distinctly says that his object is to secure the Canons against such spoliations as they had suffered at the hands of the Provosts.([20]) This object, there can be no doubt, was effectually compassed. When part of the estates of the church was held by the Canons in common, while each Canon held another portion as his own separate endowment, it is clear that they could no longer lie at the mercy of any one officer. He also founded an admirable system of offices in his church, which, if fully carried out, would greatly improve its discipline within and greatly extend its usefulness without. But there can be no doubt that his changes had indirectly, and certainly undesignedly, another effect of which we cannot so fully approve, the effect of weakening the old connexion between the Bishop and his cathedral church. We must remember that a spirit of corporate isolation was the spirit of the times. Liberty, as has been well said, meant privilege. Every body of men, ecclesiastical or civil, strove rather for its own independence than for the wellbeing of the whole country. Every town, district, monastery, university, ecclesiastical body of any kind, did all it could to procure exemptions of one kind or another, to withdraw itself from the general and ordinary jurisdiction and to set up some exceptional jurisdiction of its own. Traces of this system linger here and there, wherever there is a temporal jurisdiction different from the jurisdiction of the ordinary Judges and magistrates, wherever there is an ecclesiastical jurisdiction different from that of the Archbishop, the Bishop, and their regular officers. I am far from saying that the working of this system has been altogether bad. In many cases it has been conspicuously good. For it was simply by one application of this system that the boroughs of England each, one by one, wrested or bought their independence from their temporal or spiritual lords. But it illustrates the difference between those times and ours that the original independence of those boroughs was won by a series of isolated local struggles, while their reform in our days was wrought by a single Act of Parliament for the whole country. The spirit of local and corporate independence was the natural, and in many cases the beneficial, result of the circumstances of the time. But it had its weak side, especially in ecclesiastical matters. The monasteries set the example in obtaining exemptions from the jurisdiction of the Bishop of the diocese. Other ecclesiastical corporations followed them. Each cathedral Chapter now became a distinct corporation, with a head, in the person of its Dean, distinct from the Bishop. I suspect that the institution of the Deanery, more than any of the other changes, tended to weaken the tie between Bishop and his Chapter. Hitherto the Bishop had been the head of his Canons, much as an Abbot was the head of his monks. Now the Chapter became a separate body, with interests and possessions of its own distinct from those of the Bishop. It had a head of its own, who must have been strongly tempted to set himself up as a rival of the Bishop. The old tie was gradually loosened; the Bishop, from being the immediate head of his cathedral, sank into the mere Visitor of an independent corporation, having less authority in his own church than in any other church in the diocese. It became a point of honour with capitular bodies to lay more stress on maintaining their chartered rights against the Bishop than on working with the Bishop to promote the ends for which both Bishops and Chapters were founded. The Bishop and his Chapter became alike isolated. Two authorities which were intended to work together very much like a King and his Parliament, silently divided the departments of administration between them. The Bishop came to manage the affairs of the diocese without any reference to the advice of his nominal Council the Chapter. The Chapter came to manage the affairs of the cathedral with very little reference to the authority of the Bishop. Instead of an immediate ruler, he became an external power, called in ever and anon to reform an abuse or to settle a dispute. It gradually came, in most places at least, to be held in law that the freehold of the cathedral church was vested in the Dean and Chapter or Prior and Convent. The old theory that, when the cathedral was served by monks, the Bishop was their Abbot, had thus quite died away. At the dissolution of religious houses, the monastic cathedrals were surrendered by their Priors and Convents, just like the other monasteries. The metropolitan church of England became the property of Henry the Eighth, and he had the right in law, not only, as he did, to despoil it of all its treasures, but to destroy, dismantle, or desecrate the fabric itself, as was actually done with the churches of Bath and Coventry. The Bishop of Coventry and Lichfield earnestly prayed that his head church might be spared, but the tyrant was not to be moved, and in law, as law had gradually come to be understood, no right of the Bishop was touched by its destruction.([21])

Thus the Chapter of Wells gradually became, like other Chapters, no longer a body of clerks headed by the Bishop, but a separate corporation subject only to the Bishop's visitation. But this was not the only instance of the spirit of local and corporate isolation which is supplied by the history of capitular bodies. Besides the Chapter becoming an independent corporation aggregate, we have seen that each Canon became for some purposes a separate corporation sole, independent alike of the Bishop and of his brother Canons. Nor did this independence always affect matters of property only. The notions of property and jurisdiction were closely connected in the ideas of those times. It followed that in many cases the parishes where either the Chapter or any particular Prebendary had property, those especially where they possessed advowsons or rectories, became exempt from the ordinary jurisdiction of the Bishop, and were placed under the peculiar jurisdiction of the Chapter itself or of the particular Prebendary.([22]) My friend the Sub-Dean can bear witness that, though his rectory and advowson have gone elsewhere, he still retains, or very lately retained, some small remnants of ecclesiastical jurisdiction among my neighbours at Wookey. But the spirit of corporate independence went further still. We have not yet come to the days of Vicars and Chantry-priests. But we shall find that even these purely subordinate officers, mere assistants to the Canons as regards their ecclesiastical duties, became perfectly independent corporations as regards their temporal possessions.

I have dwelt at length on the changes wrought by Bishop Robert in the constitution of the foundation, because they were the beginning of the constitution as it still exists, and because these changes of Bishop Robert's were simply one example out of many of the changes which were going on everywhere. The

constitution which was assumed by the church of
Wells was essentially the same as the constitution
which was assumed by all the secular cathedrals, some
a little sooner, some a little later. The exact number
and functions of the officers are not everywhere precisely the same. But we everywhere find the Precentor,
the most absolutely indispensable functionary of all,
and we commonly find the Dean, Chancellor, and
Treasurer. The distinction too between the property
of the Chapter as a body and the property of separate
Prebendaries is common to all the cathedrals of the
Old Foundation.

I now come to what Bishop Robert did with regard
to the fabric of the church. I have already said,
while speaking of Robert's building at Bath, that our
two chief accounts, earlier and later, do not exactly
agree as to the extent of his works at either place.
The earlier account seems to assert a complete rebuilding from the ground; the later implies only a
thorough repair of a church which had become ruinous and dangerous.([23]) As all the work of this date at
Wells has vanished, it is impossible to say for certain
how the case really stood, but at all events Robert's
repair must have been very extensive, as it was followed
by a reconsecration of the church. But what I want
you specially to remark is this, that the church which
Robert either repaired or destroyed in order to rebuild must have been the Old-English church, one can
hardly venture to say the church of Ine, but very
possibly the church of Eadward the Elder. The old
church thus lasted, certainly to the middle of the
twelfth century, perhaps even some way into the

thirteenth. Now at either of those times large churches earlier than the Norman Conquest must have been almost as rare in England as they are now. The Norman and other foreign Prelates, who were thrust into English Bishopricks and Abbeys, had almost everywhere rebuilt their minsters in the newly imported style long before the time of Robert's episcopate. But it is plain that such was not the case at Wells. The acts of Gisa and John of Tours are so fully recorded that, if either of them had rebuilt the church of Wells, we could not fail to have heard of it. Gisa, we know, thought poorly of the building,(24) but he does not say that he did anything to improve or enlarge it. His architectural works were all devoted to the accommodation of the Canons on his new system. And it is plain from the account of his burial that he was buried in the same church in which his predecessor lay, which it therefore follows that he had not rebuilt. John of Tours, I need not say, was not likely to rebuild the church of Wells. In short, we have no mention of the actual fabric of the cathedral till we come across this description of its dangerous and ruinous state in Robert's time. The Old-English church was therefore still standing, and, if Robert merely repaired and did not wholly rebuild, parts of it must have been standing down to the great rebuilding under Jocelin. Perhaps we may be the more inclined to think that this was the case, when we see how soon Robert's work was done, and when we remember how utterly his work was swept away so soon after his own time. The church was consecrated in the presence of three other Bishops, one of whom,

Robert, Bishop of Hereford, died in 1148.(²⁵) Our Robert therefore had at the outside only thirteen years of the stormy reign of Stephen for the rebuilding of his church at Wells, and that at a time when he was also occupied with his architectural works at Bath, and with his efforts to recover the lost property of the Canons. At all events, whatever was the exact extent of his work, it is certain that not a single bit of detail of his age is to be seen in the present church; a single stone with Norman mouldings, which must have formed part of Robert's building, is built up in the house which was lately restored by Mr. Parker. That is literally all; in the church itself I think I can show one small bit of masonry of Robert's age, but it is merely masonry, without any ornamental work. It is seldom that one of the massive piles of that day has so utterly gone, without leaving any trace of itself. But it is easy to call up before our eyes what the church of Robert must have been. It was small compared with the great Romanesque minsters of Peterborough, Ely, and Norwich, or with its own rival at Bath. The present building is one of the very smallest of the original cathedral churches of England, and, as it stood in Robert's day, it must have been much smaller than it is now. The western limb was most likely of its present length; the eastern limb was very much shorter than it now is, containing probably only one or two bays and the apse. The choir—the place for the stalls—if not actually placed in the western limb, was under the central tower, the usual place for it in Norman minsters. It has indeed struck me that what Robert did was perhaps mainly to rebuild and enlarge the choir and presbytery,—a change which the increase in the number of the Canons would make needful, and which, as changing the site of the high altar, would call for a fresh hallowing of the building. In this case it is quite possible that the ancient nave may have remained substantially untouched down to the building of the present church. As for the style of Robert's building, whatever he built or added was of course built in the fully developed Norman style of the middle of the twelfth century, somewhat less massive, somewhat more highly enriched, than the church of John de Villulâ at Bath is likely to have been. But the style was essentially the same; the church of Eadward at Westminster was still the great model for English buildings;([26]) it is not likely that the pointed arch found its way, even as a purely constructive feature, into any part of the church of Robert. If the nave or any other considerable part of the ancient minster really survived, it would have been most curious to trace the way in which the architect, like the architects of Le Mans and of Saint Remigius at Rheims, doubtless strove to throw a coating of the more refined Romanesque of his own day over the still living body of the old primitive building. But on these matters we cannot get beyond fairly probable conjecture. Whatever stood before the days of Robert, whatever was built in the days of Robert, has utterly vanished. Still there does seem every reason to believe that the ancient church of Wells, a church most likely of the tenth century, remained at least to the middle of the twelfth century, and that large portions of it were not improbably standing even in the thirteenth.

The episcopal reign of Bishop Robert has thus occupied a large part of our time. Nor has it done so unworthily, for his episcopate is the most important of all in the constitutional history of the Church of Wells; and, though all Robert's architectural works happen to have perished, yet his episcopate must have been almost equally important with regard to the material fabric. We may pass more lightly over the time of the two Bishops who came between the first great founder Robert and the second great founder Jocelin. Their time is a most important time in the history of the see of Bath and Wells; it is the most important of all times in the later history of the Church of Glastonbury; but it provides but little matter bearing on the history of either the fabric or the constitution of the Church of Wells. Bishop Robert died in 1166, and the see remained vacant for seven years. The next Bishop, Reginald, founded several new prebends,([27]) but I do not find any mention of the fabric in his time. Then came the famous Savaric, the last of our Lotharingian Prelates, whose detailed history belongs in a special manner to Professor Stubbs.([28]) His great object, as we all know, was to annex the Abbey of Glastonbury to the Bishoprick, and to make Glastonbury a third, or perhaps rather the first, cathedral church of the Diocese.([29]) The controversy which arose about this matter fills up the whole of his episcopate, and part of that of his successor, Jocelin, who was Bishop from 1206 to 1242. For a short time Glastonbury, much against the will of its own monks, remained an episcopal see, with the Bishop for its Abbot, and Jocelin himself signs the Great Charter by the title of Bishop of Bath and Glastonbury. One might have thought that this change was one which tended still more to the lowering of the position of the Church of Wells. But we may perhaps infer that it was not so taken, as we find the Dean and some of the Canons of Wells acting zealously on the Bishop's side in the course of the long dispute.([30]) In the end, as is well known, the monks of Glastonbury gained their point at the expense of considerable sacrifices. Jocelin gave up his claims over the Abbey; the Bishop of Bath and Wells ceased to be Bishop and Abbot of Glastonbury, and the minster of Glastonbury ceased to be a cathedral church. It became once more simply a monastery governed by its own Abbot, as it had been for so many ages. On the other hand, the monks of Glastonbury had to buy their independence by the surrender of several manors and advowsons; and, though the Bishop ceased to be Abbot, yet he retained a more efficient right of visitation over the Abbey than Bishops could commonly retain over monasteries so great in wealth and dignity.([31]) This agreement was made in the year 1218, and from that time till Jocelin's death in 1242, it would seem that his chief attention was given to the rebuilding of the fabric of the church of Wells, to some further changes in the constitution of the Chapter, and to other good works in the city. He could not have begun his works at Wells before the year 1211; for the first five years of his episcopate were spent in banishment under the tyranny of John.([32]) Jocelin was a Wells man in every sense of the word. As he is called Jocelin of Wells, and as his brother Hugh, Bishop of Lincoln, is called Hugh of Wells, both were doubtless natives of the city, and Jocelin had been a Canon of the Church before he became its Bishop. He is a memorable man indeed in our local history; he may be called the creator of the cathedral as it now stands, he put the last finishing touches to the capitular constitution devised by Robert, and he also began another of our institutions which has lasted to our own time, I mean that of the Vicars. With regard to the fabric, I now come upon ground which Professor Willis has made his own. As many of you doubtless remember, he has twice lectured on Wells Cathedral: once in 1851, when the Archæological Institute at their Bristol meeting paid a hurried visit to Wells; and again in 1863, at the meeting of our own local Archæological and Natural History Society, an honour, let me tell you, of a very rare kind, and which I believe has not been granted to any other local society. Now, if we had Professor Willis's lecture as he delivered it, there would be little else for any future historian of the fabric to do except to make spoil of what the Professor said. But unluckily, the great work of which this and all other Professor Willis's lectures of the same kind were to form parts has not yet appeared, and I greatly fear that it never will appear. We have therefore to draw our own recollections, helped by the report in our own Society's Proceedings, 1863, which is at least fuller and more accurate than that in the Bristol volume of the Institute. I shall therefore, in what I have to say as to architectural facts, follow Professor Willis as nearly as I can, though I shall have to make more use of my own light than I need have done if I really had the Professor's lecture before me. I speak thus of architectural facts, with regard to which he who follows Professor Willis will seldom go wrong; as for matters of taste and opinion, architectural or otherwise, I hold myself independent of Professor Willis as of every other man. But I should add that I have not had, like the Professor, the advantage of a diligent study of the manuscript documents in possession of the Chapter. I once glanced at them in company with Professor Stubbs, and that is all. When these documents are printed, as all documents of the kind ought to be printed, I hope I may be able to make good use of them; but while they are shut up in manuscript they are useless to me. Searching into manuscripts is a special gift, one which Professor Willis and Professor Stubbs, and some nearer to ourselves, possess in the highest degree, but it is a work for which I have neither time nor inclination.

Let us now look, in a general historical way, without attempting to enter into any very minute detail, at the church of Wells, as it was designed and begun, if not absolutely finished, during the long episcopate of Jocelin. That episcopate reached over twenty-four years from the settlement of the Glastonbury controversy, over thirty-six from Jocelin's first consecration. That any part of the church is older than Jocelin I see no reason to believe; but if anybody holds that the porch may be a little earlier than his time, I will not dispute against him. The church of Jocelin, thus understood, takes in the nave, the transepts, and what is now the choir proper, that is, the three western arches of the eastern limb. It takes in the three towers, up to the point where they rise above the roof of the church, but no higher. With the present presbytery, that is, the three eastern bays of the eastern limb, with the Lady chapel and the other small eastern chapels, with the Chapter-house and the tops of the towers, we have as yet nothing to do. Now within these limits, that is, between the west door and the Bishop's throne, I think that every one of common observation must have remarked that there are two styles of architecture in use. I do not speak of certain small changes and insertions made at later times, such as the tracery which has been put into the nave windows, or of the changes which were made when it was found needful to add new props to the great central tower. Of these I shall have to speak further on. I speak of differences of style in the original fabric itself. The west front, within and without, differs widely in its architectural detail from the arcades of the nave and transepts. If there is any one here who has never remarked the difference, I can only say, let him go into the church to-morrow and use his eyes for himself. Both parts are built in the style which is called Gothic, the style which uses pointed arches with an appropriate form of ornament; both are built in that variety of Gothic which is called Lancet or Early English, that is, the first form of Gothic, which in England is mainly distinguished by the use of long narrow windows without tracery. But, notwithstanding this general likeness, there is a wide difference between the two. To those who have never marked the difference I am not sure that I could make it perfectly intelligible, except either on the spot or with the help of large drawings. But go, I say, into the building itself, go especially under either of the western towers, at the point where the two styles join, and I think any one of common observation will easily see the difference. The west front is built in that form of Early Gothic which is common in other parts of England, the style of Ely, Lincoln, and Salisbury. The rest of the Early work is built in a style which in England is almost peculiar to Somersetshire, South Wales, and the neighbouring counties, and which is much more like French work. Among greater churches it is the style of Glastonbury and Llandaff as well as of Wells; among smaller buildings good examples will be found in parts of Whitchurch in Somersetshire and Cheriton in Gower, and above all in the beautiful church of Slymbridge in Gloucestershire. Of the two styles used in this part of the building this is the one which, speaking of England generally, we should be inclined to call foreign, and the other native. Here in the West we must call the ordinary English style of Ely and Salisbury foreign, and the French-looking style of Wells and Llandaff we must call native or local. Our local Somersetshire and South-Welsh style has a good deal of the earlier Romanesque leaven hanging about it; its mouldings and the clustering of its pillars are much less free; the abaci or tops of the capitals are square or octagonal instead of round; it makes no use of those detached shafts, often of marble, which are so abundantly found in the west front. Now which of these two is the older? The local style is no doubt older in idea; but that does not absolutely prove that the parts of the church which are built in it are necessarily older in date. The evidence of the masonry is puzzling; some bits look one way and some the other. Mr. Parker and I once looked very carefully at it, and we were both inclined to think that the west front was the oldest part, that it had been built up against the earlier church, like the west front of Peterborough, and that the nave and the rest had been built later. Then Professor Willis came and told us that we were wrong, and showed us other signs to prove that the west front was the latest part built. We of course dutifully bowed to our master; but, if the west front is the latest part, then it follows, what Professor Willis is inclined to doubt, that the whole work was finished during the episcopate of Jocelin—and surely thirty-one years is enough even for so great a work. For that Jocelin built the west front I have no doubt at all. It is certain that he built the oldest parts of the palace at Wells and of the manor-house at Wookey ([33]), and the style in both of those buildings exactly agrees with the foreign style of the west front, and not with the local style of the nave. And these buildings are certainly earlier than some works in the local style. For it is certain from an account in Matthew Paris that in 1248, six years after Jocelin's death, the vault, which was not commonly put on till some time after the walls and arches were finished, was then being put on some part of the church of Wells. The vault fell in by reason of an earthquake and did a good deal of damage.([34]) The present vault then is later than Jocelin, and to the repair rendered needful by this accident I am also inclined to attribute the breaks and style of differences—not amounting to differences of style—which it is easy to see between the eastern and western bays of the nave. The chances therefore seem on the whole to be that Jocelin began to build in the local style; that for his later works, the west front and the two houses at Wells and Wookey, he sent for architects from a distance, who brought in the more advanced style which was usual in other parts of England; but that the mere damage caused by the fall of the vault was, even after his death, repaired by the local workmen in the local style.

This last work was almost certainly done after Jocelin's time; still it was simply the restoration of a damaged portion of his design, and it does not at all bar his claim to be looked on as the real builder of the church. The church was hallowed in 1239. This shows that so much of the building as was absolutely needful for divine service was then finished. It does not prove whether the other parts were finished or not, neither does it show how long the essential parts had been finished at the time of the consecration. For in the history of those times we often come across complaints that various churches still remained unconsecrated, and indeed Mr. Dimock has told me that the present church of Lincoln has never been consecrated to this day. We find several cases in which a whole batch of cathedral and abbey churches were consecrated in the same year, and this year 1239 is one of those cases. In that year, besides the cathedral church of Wells, seven great abbey churches were all consecrated.(35) This date therefore proves only that the choir was ready for service in 1239. It proves nothing either way as to the state of the works in the rest of the church, and it does not prove that the choir may not have been ready some years before. But we can thus see how much at least of the church was finished in that year. The choir was no doubt under the tower, stretching possibly a bay eastward or a bay westward. For you must remember that it is the only three western bays of the eastern limb which belong to Jocelin's work. It is quite impossible that the whole choir and presbytery could have been crammed into the narrow space of those three bays. It follows then that the eastern limb contained only the presbytery, that is, the void space left to give dignity to the high altar, while the choir proper, containing the stalls of the Canons, must still have kept its old place under the central tower. By this time then the presbytery, the tower-choir, and the transepts must all have been finished, together with at least one or two bays of the nave, to form at once a constructive abutment to the tower and a necessary approach to the choir. The work of Jocelin's date in the transepts and eastern limb differs in some small points of detail, especially in the triforium, from the work in the nave. There is no difference in style, no difference in general effect, but these are just those little differences which show that they were not all built at exactly the same time. In a work which may well have been spread over thirty-one years it is not wonderful if there were several stoppages and fresh beginnings. And of such a stoppage and fresh beginning we may see clear signs at this particular point of the building. Every one who looks carefully at the buttresses of the north aisle of the nave will see that, though the general effect of all is the same, yet at two different points there are minute differences, showing change or stoppage of work. One of these points is where I have just mentioned, at the second bay from the east. This no doubt marks the completion of the first part of the work, the part absolutely necessary for divine service. The other marks the extent of the repair caused by the fall of the vault. When the first or absolutely necessary part of the work was done, a stoppage of a few years might well take place, and it is well to try and call up before our eyes the appearance of the church during this interval. The old nave—probably, as we have seen, the Old-English nave recast by Robert—still remained in the greater part of its extent; it would be taken down piecemeal as the new nave gradually stretched itself westward. For a short time therefore the old nave, much lower no doubt as well as much ruder in style than the new work, must have stood against it in an incongruous fashion. The eastern limb, the transepts, and the small part of the nave that was built, must have soared like a tower over the older part. This is a state of things which we do not often see in England, but which is common enough in France, and which reaches its height in the famous cathedral of Beauvais.

There the old nave of the tenth century—the *Basse
Œuvre* as it is locally called—still survives—at least
it survived while I was there,—cleaving as a kind of
excrescence to the mighty pile which has risen up
to the east of it. And with the reverse process we
are familiar enough in England, and specially familiar
in our own shire. It is a characteristic of the churches
of Somersetshire that the nave has often been rebuilt on a lofty and magnificent scale, while the choir
still remains small, low, and quite unworthy of its
companion. We may see this disproportion to some
extent in our own church of Saint Cuthbert, and it
comes out much more strongly at Yatton and in some
other of the great parish churches of the county. At
the time of which I speak the transepts and eastern
limb of Wells Cathedral must have soared over the
nave, exactly as the nave of Yatton soars over its
transepts and eastern limb. Then the rest of the
nave would be gradually rebuilt. We have seen that
there is some slight difference of detail, not affecting
the general design, between the transepts and the eastern
part of the nave. And going westward, we can see
the place of the second stoppage, marked by a second
slight change of detail, probably caused, as I have
already said, by the fall of the vault in 1248.
Still, notwithstanding all these smaller differences,
the whole work, except the west front, is essentially
in one style, and is evidently built from one general
design. And though the repair which followed
the fall of the vault must have happened after
Jocelin was dead, yet I think we may fairly speak
of the thirteenth century work at Wells as being,

as a whole, the work of that great Prelate. This is a case in which I see no reason to depart from the received tradition and the received manner of speech.

Still, when I speak of the work as being the work of Jocelin, I ought perhaps to pause and explain, and in some sort to qualify, my meaning. As regards the design of the building, Jocelin may or may not have been his own architect. In some of our great churches there is no doubt that the Bishop, the Abbot, or some other member of the society, really was the architect. William of Wykeham, long after Jocelin's time, really designed his own nave at Winchester, but we read of some of the works in Saint Alban's Abbey that they were designed by one of the other officers of the monastery, but that it was held right to attribute them to the Abbot, on account of his higher dignity.([36]) While Jocelin's nave was building, the vault over the nave of Gloucester Abbey was actually made by the hands of the monks themselves.([37]) In other cases there can be no doubt that professional architects and masons were employed, just as they are now.([38]) The vault which fell in at Wells was being made, not by the hands of the Canons or of their Vicars, but by those of skilled workmen. One thing is certain, that the designer of the local work at Wells must have been a local man; whether he was actually Jocelin of Wells in his own person I cannot say. Another thing is equally certain, that, before the work was done, the local style was forsaken and another style was adopted in its stead. And that this was the personal act of Jocelin is shown by the new style being used, not

G

only in the west front of the church, but in his own domestic buildings both at Wells and at Wookey. And as to another point, when I call the work Jocelin's work, I do not necessarily mean that he paid out of his own pocket for everything that was done. We must remember that in Jocelin's day we are just at a moment of transition in the history of our own and of other churches. The earlier Bishops, who did what they pleased, no doubt paid for whatever they did. At any rate, we cannot suppose that the Canons of Wells in the eleventh century did, out of their poverty and beggarly estate, contribute much either towards the erection of Gisa's buildings or towards their pulling down by John of Tours. In our own day, as we all know, any works done to the cathedral are done by the Chapter, either out of their own funds, or out of funds collected by them. In the intermediate ages we sometimes find works of this sort attributed to the Bishop alone, sometimes to the Chapter alone, sometimes to the Bishop and Chapter working together. I suspect that this last would commonly be the truer account in all cases; at any rate, what either Bishop or Chapter did the other party must have consented to. Jocelin was doubtless the great mover in the work, the life and soul of the whole undertaking. The whole would be done under his care, and his personal contributions would doubtless be large. But all this in no way shuts out the co-operation of the Chapter, of the clergy and laity of the diocese, and of well-disposed persons wherever they might be found.([39])

Another part of the buildings of the church belongs

to the age of Jocelin, where his hand might not have been looked for at first. This is the cloister as it stood in its first estate. You will remember that the cloister which was built by Gisa, together with his dormitory and refectory, was pulled down by John of Tours. You will also remember that a cloister, which in a monastery is an essential part of the building, and is always built after a particular model, is in a secular church a mere convenience, which may perfectly well be left out, and which may be built in any place and after any fashion which may be thought good. Jocelin then, or his Canons, now built them a cloister, but it was a cloister which was no longer accompanied, as in Gisa's time, by any refectory or dormitory. It is more like a monastic cloister than those of Chichester and Hereford; it is less like one than that of Salisbury. It occupies, like a monastic cloister, one side of the nave; still it is not a perfect square, but an irregular parallelogram; it has no walk on the north side, and the eastern walk comes up against the south end of the transept, while in a monastery it would have been built against its western wall. To the east, where the chapter-house would have stood in a monastery, there was a detached Lady chapel, of which the traces may easily be seen, but which was rebuilt late in the fifteenth century and wholly destroyed in the sixteenth. Now that the cloister was first built at this time is plain, as all the outer walls, including that very pretty doorway leading to the Palace, are all of Jocelin's date. The doorway leading from the transept into the cloister is also mentioned in an Act of Chapter in 1297, printed in Dugdale's Monasticon. ([40])

But this very doorway, and the doorway which is in some sort the fellow to it in the south-western tower, give us the surest signs that the cloister is not now in the same state in which it was originally designed. Even in its first estate, it seems to have been, as we should expect, an addition, though an addition made not very long after the building of the part of the church which it joins. The wall comes up uncomfortably close against this fine doorway, though it does not mutilate it in the way which is done by the vault which was added long after. This vault, and the window-tracery of the cloister of the same date, are therefore not only later additions, but additions which could not have been so much as contemplated when the cloister was first built. What then was the cloister in its original state? That its outer wall was of stone is plain; but I believe that whatever was inside, the roof and whatever there may have been in the way of tracery or arcading, was of wood. Wooden cloisters were not uncommon. Even in so great a monastery as Glastonbury, it is plain that the cloister was not of stone.

Jocelin, the great builder of the fabric, is hardly less memorable with regard to the constitution of the church. He put the last touches to the system which had been devised by Robert. To him, as we have seen, was perhaps owing the foundation of the other dignities besides the two chief ones, the Deanery and the Precentorship. He certainly increased the number of prebends, and enlarged or settled again the endowments of some of them.([11]) And to him is owing the beginning of another class among the officers of our church, who still remain among us; I mean the Vicars. The institution of this order is closely connected with certain changes which were going on about this time in our own and in other capitular bodies, and which produced the distinction which I have already mentioned, and with which we are all familiar, between Residentiary and Non-residentiary Canons. All the old capitular bodies were framed upon one general model, the essential features of which they retain to this day. But, amid this general likeness, each church has its own personal peculiarities; it would be impossible to find two Old Foundation cathedrals in England which are exactly alike in the names, numbers, and duties of their officers. And so with the change of which I am now about to speak; it happened in all the secular cathedrals with the single exception of Llandaff; but it was not brought about in all by exactly the same stages nor at exactly the same time. The general result was the same in all; but the process was not everywhere the same, and this or that change might be made a few years earlier in one place and a few years later in another. The exact dates and stages in the church of Wells I am not prepared to tell you, till all the information which now lurks in manuscript has been unlocked by means of the printing-press. There is one among us who has no doubt mastered every single record in its existing form, and who, I feel sure, can tell us the year, day, and hour of every change of detail. But all I can do is to point out the stages of change in a general way, and to mark that in the time of Jocelin the changes of which I speak were at least beginning.

I have already spoken of that inveterate tendency to pluralities, and consequently to non-residence, which was the bane of the mediæval Church, and which brought to nothing so many fair schemes of discipline and reform. This had already begun to extend itself to cathedral foundations. We may be sure that in early times the whole body of Canons were constantly resident. Gisa at all events, we may be sure, would allow of no absentees from the common refectory and the common dormitory. But the changes made by Robert would certainly tend to make non-residence possible. A Canon was no longer a mere member of a body which, even as a body, had hardly any corporate rights. His prebend had now been made a distinct benefice, as independent, as far as its temporal possessions went, as a Bishoprick or a rectory. The feudal ideas which, as I before said, came to be applied to ecclesiastical benefices, would come to be applied to a prebend no less than to a Bishoprick or a rectory. It would come to be looked on as a benefice, which a man might, as in the case of any other benefice, hold along with any other preferment, and, as in the case of any other benefice, its holder would deem his conscience discharged if its duties were discharged by deputy. The non-residence of Canons became a matter of complaint in the twelfth century. It was a favourite subject for monkish writers, who naturally found in it a fruitful field for declamation against their secular rivals. Thus Richard of Devizes, one of the most amusing writers of that or of any age, holds forth on the superiority of the monks who praised God with their own mouths, while the Canons praised Him only through the mouths of their Vicars. He goes on to draw a grotesque picture of a stranger coming to ask alms at the door of a rich Canon. The door is opened by a poor Vicar, who bids the wayfaring man go away, as the master of the house is not at home.([42]) Then, at a somewhat earlier time, in the Life of Saint Thomas of Canterbury, we find how the man whom he sent over with a bull of excommunication against the Bishop of London went to high mass in Saint Paul's Cathedral on so great a festival as the Ascension, and found the officiating priest to be neither Bishop, Dean, nor Canon, but only a Vicar.([43]) An incidental notice of this sort speaks volumes.

The non-residence of the Canons was in itself an evil, and it grew out of a relaxation of discipline; still it wrought some incidental good by calling into being a class of men whom I look upon as highly valuable, and indeed as essential to the proper working of the cathedral system. I mean the Non-residentiary Canons. The distinction between Residentiary and Non-residentiary Canons, which is found in all the strictly English cathedrals of the Old Foundation, grew up in different churches at nearly the same time and by nearly the same steps, but with some differences of detail in each case. The first stage seems to have been one of very general non-residence. The Canons lived at the cathedral or not just as they pleased; those who did not reside keeping (as we have incidentally heard) Vicars to discharge their share of the duties of the church. Here we have the origin of that body of Vicars, clerical and lay, whom we still see among us. The Vicar at first was simply the deputy of the Canon whose place he took, just as a curate takes the place of a non-resident rector. Each Vicar was thus dependent on a particular Canon, who was looked upon as his *Master*. Of this name, after the lapse of so many ages and after such great changes in the position of the Vicars, we still have traces among us. Among the legislative acts of Jocelin were some which concerned the institution of Vicars.([44]) He certainly did not form them into a corporation, which was the work of a benefactor of the next age. But he probably insisted that the non-residence of the Canons should not involve any neglect of the services of the church, that every absent Canon should be represented by a competent Vicar, perhaps even that each Vicar should receive a decent stipend. It is plain that the principle of non-residence was already recognized. Savaric, in founding two new prebends in the church, had directed them to be held by the Abbots of Muchelney and Athelney for the time being.([45]) It probably was good policy thus to connect the heads of two great monastic houses in the diocese with the diocesan church. But it is plain that the two Abbots were not meant to reside permanently at Wells. They would have their votes in Chapter, and they would come to give them on fitting occasions; but their share in the ordinary duties of the cathedral must have been discharged by deputy from the beginning.

Non-residence thus became rife everywhere. But strict men naturally looked upon it as a scandal. It was not fitting that all or most of the responsible officers of the church should be habitually absent from their post, leaving their duties to be discharged by deputy. And it is likely enough that the deputies might not in every case be the most creditable representatives of their principals that could be found. It was needful to take some steps to check the system by which, in cathedral churches as well as elsewhere, one man did the work while another took the pay. On the other hand, we can see a growing and very reasonable feeling that, as it was not possible, so neither was it desirable, to demand constant residence at the cathedral from the whole of so large a body as the Canons had now become. Now that the prebends had been increased to so great a number as fifty, there was really no object in requiring the holders of all of them to be always present either in the choir or in the chapter-house. The twofold objects of the cathedral foundation would be better carried out by dividing the Canons into two classes. One portion of the body was placed constantly on the spot, to maintain the regular services and to discharge the routine duties of the corporation. Another portion consisted of men scattered about the diocese, appearing at the cathedral only at stated seasons, who, as being at once cathedral clergy and diocesan clergy, might help, above all other men, to keep up the connexion between the mother church and the diocese at large. How far these objects were consciously present to the minds of those who established the distinction between Residentiary and Non-residentiary Canons, I do not pretend to say; but I do say that the distinction has really worked for good, and has given us, in the Non-residentiary Canons, a very valuable body of men, whose position I should like to see better appreciated than it commonly is. This is, however, a subject which will again come before us, and at present we have to deal only with the origin of the distinction. In the first stage no fixed number of Residentiaries was appointed. It was open to every Canon to reside if he chose; and if he chose to reside, he was in every sense a Residentiary. There could not be then, as there is now, the strange sight of Canons, even dignitaries, of the cathedral, who really do reside, but who are not reckoned as Residentiaries, while others bear the name of Residentiaries who come among us for three months in the year only. The first stage was commonly this. Every Canon could reside or not, as he pleased; but those who did reside enjoyed great worldly advantages over those who did not. The common revenues of the corporation were divided among those only who resided, while those who did not reside received only, what the corporation of course could not meddle with, the incomes of their own prebends. The non-resident thus had only his prebend; the resident had his prebend and a share in the common income as well. This is all explained in a statute of Jocelin himself, dated in 1242, the year of his death, in which a daily distribution is ordered to such Canons and Vicars as are present, while at the end of the year the remainder of the common revenues is to be divided among such Canons as have kept residence. Residence is defined to be six months in the year for a simple Canon, that is, for one not a dignitary, and eight for the Dean, Precentor, Chancellor, and Treasurer.([46])

With this stage, when residence was voluntary, is connected the curious institution of *ribs*, which, as far as I know, is peculiar to our own church. A rib, as many of you know, is a house, or a piece of ground fit for building a house, which the Bishop must give to some Canon, but which he might give to any Canon that he pleased. If therefore the Bishop wished to call into residence any Canon who had not a house of his own, he might give him the means of residing by giving him a rib. At this stage, then, residence was optional, just as it is at this moment among Fellows of Colleges in the Universities. But there was this important difference, that the resident Canon, unlike the resident Fellow, greatly bettered his income by residing. The natural result was that, whereas hitherto the tendency had been to shirk residence, there now was a general rush of the Canons to reside. And this new tendency to residence next led to all kinds of devices to hinder residence. If a small number were already residing, and therefore divided the common fund among them, they would be tempted to look with no friendly eye on those of their brethren who came trooping in to share their funds, and thereby to lessen their own dividends. It was often ordered that no one should be allowed to reside, or at least to draw any profits from his residence, unless he obtained the consent of those who were already Residentiaries. And it was no uncommon rule, a rule which existed in our own church, that no one should reside unless he purchased the right to residence by giving a series of costly entertainments to his brother Canons and to various other people.([47]) This of course many of the Canons could not afford to do, and so were hindered from residing if they wished. All these devices were clear abuses, arising out of a selfish wish on the part of the existing Residentiaries to have as few sharers in their dividends as they could. Still it was clearly not to be wished that the whole body of Canons should reside, while it was desirable that the choice of those who should reside should not depend upon their power of giving great dinners. The remedy was to appoint a fixed number of Residentiaries to be chosen in some regular way out of the whole body of Canons. This was done sooner or later in all the strictly English Old Foundation churches, but the number of the Residentiaries, and the way of choosing them from among the Canons, differed widely in different places. Here in Wells the number finally settled was eight, including the Dean; now, by the Act of Parliament settling such matters, it is, as you all know, four besides the Dean. Here too, on a vacancy among the Residentiaries, the existing Residentiary body determines which of the other Canons shall be called into residence. You will see that the rule that no man could reside without the consent of the existing Residentiaries would, as soon as there was a fixed number, naturally grow into an election of this kind. But in some places, as at York, the Dean alone called into residence whom he would. In others, as at Lincoln, the duty of residence was laid on some or all of the dignitaries, who of course must reside if they are to do their duties effectually. This, you will see, was in effect to put the choice of Residentiaries into the hands of the Bishop. At Saint David's this mode was combined with that with which we are familiar here. There was a Residentiary body of six, consisting of three dignitaries, the Precentor, the Chancellor, and the Treasurer, and of three other Canons elected by the Residentiary body. As the Church of Saint David's had no Dean, the Precentor was the President of the Chapter.(48) These small differences meet us everywhere, but the general system is the same everywhere. Both the likeness and the unlikeness were exactly what was to be looked for, when the same causes were working in different places in a great number of institutions of the same class, but where the changes were made, not by any one general enactment, but by independent local legislators laying down rules for their own societies only. But the general result was everywhere the same. A smaller body arose within the general body of the Canons, a body on whom alone fell the duty of residence and the common daily care of the fabric and its services. The change was undoubtedly a good one. It brought in a regular order and discipline instead of a state of things which must have been verging on anarchy. It produced two classes of men, the Residentiary and the Non-residentiary Canons, each of whom, as it seems to me, has a very useful function to perform in the economy of the Church. But it had its weak side also. The tendency of a smaller body, more constantly present on the spot and more constantly in the habit of acting together, has naturally been gradually to draw all power into its own hands. The result has been that in many churches, including our own, the rights of the Non-residentiary Canons have been cut down, greatly to the disadvantage of the institution as a whole, to little beyond a bare name and a barren precedence.

I need hardly say that when the duty of residence was laid exclusively on a certain number of the Canons on behalf of the whole, it was meant that those on whom the duty of residence was laid should really discharge that duty. But the same tendencies which had before worked in the general body of Canons began after a while to work again in the smaller body of Residentiaries. It was clearly intended, it was implied in the very distinction between Residentiaries and Non-residentiaries, that those who were to reside should really reside; that the cathedral should be their home, their dwelling-place, at least as constantly as the parish of a clergyman who resides on his living is his dwelling-place. But a passion which seems almost inherent in human nature, the passion for shirking one's own immediate duties, soon stepped in. Residence was shirked even by the Residentiaries; it was cut short to the smallest possible amount, till the strange doctrine was finally established that residence was effectually kept by the presence of a single Canon, the Residentiary body coming in turn for periods which in some places fell below, and which I believe never rose above, the mystical period of three months. This period is now fixed by law for all churches alike. At Wells, however, it does seem to have been, even in the worst times, at least the theory that there should always be two Canons resident at once.([19]) But even two is a very small show out of fifty, and with what propriety of language a man who is away nine months or longer in the year can be called a Residentiary is altogether beyond my understanding. The three months' system is a mockery, and worse. Three months is too long a time for a bad man, and not long enough for a good man. The man who comes for three months only has not time enough to do much good, but he has time enough to do a great deal of mischief. We ourselves know by experience that more mischief may be done to the fabric of the cathedral in one term of three months than can, with the best will in the world, be undone in the next term. We do not want to get rid of our Residentiary Canons, but we do want to have more of their company. If our cathedrals are ever to be made what they ought to be and what they might be, the first reform of all must be that Residentiaries shall really reside. I assume of course that they hold no other preferment involving residence. I do not want them to be resident at the cathedral and non-resident somewhere else. No Dean or Canon Residentiary ought to have any other benefice, or any cure of souls, except such as may be attached to the cathedral itself. And if the right kind of men—men very far from scarce in the Church—were always made Deans and Canons Residentiary, they would find their cathedral offices enough for them, and would not go hungering after other functions which are incompatible with their proper discharge.

We must now turn once more from the constitution of the Church to its fabric. The church as built by Jocelin, though capable, as we know, of much further enlargement and improvement, was still essentially perfect. But one important building was still lacking. In a secular foundation, where each man lives in his own house, only one common building besides the church is actually necessary. The refectory and dormitory are useless; the cloister is a luxury which may be dispensed with; but there must be a place where the whole body may meet for elections, and for whatever other business they have to discharge. The Chapter-house is therefore quite as much needed in a secular as it is in a monastic foundation. And it should be noticed that in secular foundations the Chapter-house is much more strictly part of the church than it is in a monastery. In a monastery the Chapter-house is one of the main parts of the whole building. It communicates directly with the cloister, and thereby with the church and the other principal buildings. But it has no direct communication with the church; it has no more connexion with the church than the refectory has, and not nearly so much as the dormitory has. But in secular foundations the Chapter-house is much more commonly a part of the church, its principal or only entrance being from the church itself. This is a general but not an universal rule, Salisbury being a notable instance to the contrary. This, as you all know, was at first the case with the Chapter-house at Wells. When it was first built, and up to the time when the way which leads to the Vicars' Close was made, long afterwards, the only approach to the Chapter-house was from the church itself. And now that the door which leads to the Vicars' Close is always kept fastened, we may be thought to have come back again to the old state of things. Our Chapter-house is one of the best examples of a type which chiefly belongs to the thirteenth century, though one or two examples are earlier and one or two examples are later.([30]) This is the type in which the building is of an octagonal or other polygonal shape, most commonly with a single pillar in the middle, from which all the ribs of the vaulting branch out in different directions. This is the case with our own and with most other chapter-houses of this kind, both in monastic and in secular churches. But in the great example at York, and in the smaller one imitated from it at Southwell, the central pillar is wanting. With the beauty of our own Chapter-house we are all familiar; its windows are amongst the finest examples of tracery of their own date; still the details of the Chapter-house itself do not please my personal taste so much as the details, one stage earlier in the history of art, of the staircase which leads to it. The Chapter-house stands on what is commonly called a crypt, but which, as not being underground, hardly deserves that name. It is rather of a piece with those vaulted undercrofts or substructures which are so common under the principal buildings of monasteries and other houses, and which are constantly mistaken for cloisters, dormitories, and what not.([31]) There cannot be a better example than the lower stage of our own Bishop's palace. I need hardly say that, when this substructure and the staircase were made, the Chapter-house was already designed; for both staircase and substructure are simply buildings subordinate to the Chapter-house. Yet there must be a certain difference of date between the two. The staircase must be a little later than the church itself, for it is manifestly built up against the buttresses of the north transept, and, while the church has only lancet windows, the staircase has some of the best examples of the earliest form of Geometrical tracery. The Chapter-house itself again has Geometrical tracery of a later type, and the details throughout are more advanced. It appears from Professor Willis's account that in 1286 the Chapter determined to finish a certain new structure which had been long before begun, and which urgently needed to be finished. This, as the Professor says, can be no other than the Chapter-house. In 1286, then, the staircase and substructure were already finished, but the works were at a standstill, and the Chapter-house itself had not yet been begun. The result of these debates of the Chapter was the carrying out of the Chapter-house. The general design had no doubt been planned long before, and it was now carried out according to that original design, but, as might be expected, with all the changes in detail, whether we look on them as improvements or not, which had come into fashion since the work began.([52])

Thus, by the end of the thirteenth century, we may look on the church of Wells as at last finished. It still lacked much of that perfection of outline which now belongs to it, and which the next age was finally to give it. Many among that matchless group of surrounding buildings which give Wells its chief charm had not yet arisen. The church itself, with its unfinished towers, must have had a dwarfed and stunted look from every point. The Lady chapel had not yet been reared, with its apse alike to contrast with the great window of the square presbytery above it, and to group in harmony with the more lofty Chapter-house of its own form. The cloister was still of wood. The palace was still undefended by wall or moat. The Vicars' Close and its chain-bridge had not yet been dreamed of. Still the church, alike in its fabric and its constitution, may be looked on as having by this time been brought to perfection. There was still much to add, to improve, and to develope, but all that was essential was there. The church itself, though still lacking somewhat of ideal grace and finish, had been made perfect in all that was absolutely needful. The nave, recast in forms of art such as Ine and Eadward, such as Gisa and Robert, had never dreamed of, with the long range of its arcades and the soaring sweep of its newly-vaulted roof, stood, perfect from western door to rood-loft, ever ready, ever open, to welcome worshippers from city and village, from hill and combe and moor, in every corner of the land which looked to Saint Andrew's as its mother church. The choir, the stalls of the Canons, the throne of the Bishop, were still confined within the narrow space of the crossing; but that narrow space itself gave them a dignity which they lost in later arrangements. For the central lantern, not yet driven to lean on ungainly props, with the rich arcades of its upper stages still open to view, still rose, in all the simple majesty of its four mighty arches, as the noblest of canopies over the choir below. And if the receding vista of the Lady chapel, with that matchless grouping of slender pillars, that no less matchless harmony of colour, was still a thing of the future, yet we have fragments enough to tell us that the older ending of the choir was one rich with the best detail of the thirteenth century,([53]) and one which perhaps gave greater majesty to the high altar itself, the sole feature of the eastern limb, than any arrangement that can be devised with the present ground-plan. The group of buildings of which the Chapter-house now forms a part was as yet unthought of, but the great octagon itself was already rising; by the end of the century it was perhaps already finished. There it stood, with its central pillar and its surrounding stalls, the many ribs of its vault converging to one centre, typifying, as symbolical writers tell us, the government of each diocesan church, with its many members, clergy and laity, gathering around one common head and father. All this was there already; that is, everything had been done which was needful for the practical perfection of a cathedral church, though something might still be needed to give the fabric its ideal perfection as a work of art. And as with the fabric of the church, so with its constitution. The relations of the original centre of the diocese with its sister or rival churches, in one sense more ancient, in another newer than itself,([54]) had been finally and peacefully settled. The relations between the Bishop and his Chapter, between the Chapter and its subordinate officers, had been definitely settled also. All the great offices of the church which still exist had been already founded, and those duties had been attached to them which, however much they have been forgotten, still remain the duties of their holders as much now as they were then. In short, the church of Wells, alike in its fabric and in its constitution, was already perfect. The thirteenth century had done its great creative work, and had left to future ages only to improve and develope according to the principles which the thirteenth century had laid down. That is to say, the thirteenth century had done for the local church of Wells what it did for England, what it did for Europe and for the world. It is well to mark how exactly the most striking periods in our local history fall in with the great and decisive epochs in the general history of our country. The church of Wells first arose at the bidding of the first great West-Saxon lawgiver, the prince whose reign fixed for ever that the south-western peninsula of Britain should be, in speech and allegiance, if not wholly in blood, a Teutonic and not a Celtic land. The church received its Bishop at the hands of the great West-Saxon conqueror, at the moment when Wessex finally grew into England, and the first endowment of the Bishoprick of Somersetshire was a gift from the hand of the prince to whom the Northumbrian, the Scot, and the Briton bowed as their father and their lord. The old dynasty passed away and strangers sat on the throne of England; that was the time when a stranger prelate first brought into our church the foreign and novel discipline which he had learned in his own land beyond the sea. And yet, with strangers alike on the royal throne of England and in the episcopal chair of Wells, the ancient fabric, the church of native Kings and saints and heroes, still lived on. Through the reigns of the Norman and the Angevin the ancient fabric still survived as a witness that England and her Church, conquered as they were, still preserved their national being, and would one day arise to wrest their ancient freedom from the hands of their conquerors. That ancient fabric still lived on into days when its witness was no longer needed, to days when England had won her conquerors to her heart, and had changed the sons of her oppressors into the foremost champions of her freedom. A Prelate who had suffered banishment at the hands of John, whose name stands subscribed to the Great Charter of our rights, might venture to sweep away the still abiding monument which told of the older freedom of the days of Ine and Eadward. And, even before his time, we may see how the darker and brighter days of the church of Wells coincided with the darker and brighter days of England. It was during the blackest night of oppression, in the days of the tyrant Rufus, that the name of our church was for a moment wiped out from the roll of Bishopricks, and that its ministers were reduced to beggary by the arbitrary violence of a foreign Bishop. The wrong was redressed in days which, if days of sorrow and conflict, were still days of hope. If the fabric of the church was renewed and strengthened during the civil wars of Stephen, its constitution was finally settled and confirmed when peace and order returned under the sway of the great Henry. And next came the great age of all, the age which, in its creative and in its destructive power, was to leave its mark on every land from one end of heaven to the other. Time would fail to tell of all the mighty men and mighty deeds which are crowded more thickly into the age of Innocent and Frederick, the age of Saint Ferdinand and Saint Lewis, the age of Bacon and Dante, the age in distant lands of the first Mongol and the first Ottoman invaders, than into almost any other equal space in the world's history. Throughout the world destruction and creation were marching side by side; old systems were falling, new systems were rising. But it was in England alone that the new and the old could be worked together into harmony, that the age which elsewhere was an age of destruction and of creation could become simply an age of reform and restoration, an age which put new life into old names and old traditions, and made England England once again. We see the sons of the soil, of whatever blood, alike the children of the conquerors and the children of the conquered, rising in their strength to put a bridle on the tyranny of Popes and Kings, to break the yoke of the stranger, and to win the land back once more for its own children. Then it was that our tongue, our laws, our constitution, assumed those shapes which the six ages that have followed have had only to improve in detail. It was the age of Stephen Langton and Robert Fitzwalter, of Robert Grosseteste and Simon of Montfort, of Roger Bigod and Humfrey Bohun, and of the King from whom they won our freedom. And we in this place may add to the list the name of our local worthy, foremost in local honour and not without his share in the general history of our land, the rebuilder of the fabric of our church, the final lawgiver of its constitution, the honoured name of Jocelin of Wells. As it was throughout all England, so it was in our little city at the foot of Mendip. The older state of things was passing into a newer by a process of gradual and peaceful change and developement. And as throughout all England Englishmen were rising against foreign influence in every shape, so here too it was no stranger from Tours or Lüttich, but a true son of the soil, a native of the kingdom, of the shire, of the city itself, bearing the name of the city as his distinctive surname, to whom fell the great work of calling the fabric of the church into a new being, and of putting the finishing stroke to its ecclesiastical constitution. The local chronicler says with truth that there was none such before him and none such after him.([55]) Our local history contains earlier and later names which must ever claim our reverence, Beckington, Robert, Gisa himself. But no name of Canon or Dean or Bishop can dwell in the hearts of the men of Wells and Somersetshire like the man of their own shire and their own city who gave that city its greatest and most lasting ornament. He went to his rest and his works followed him; his name and his honour still abideth. Ruthless hands had, even three hundred years back, "monstrously defaced" his marble tomb within his own choir.([56]) But he is one of those who need not a marble tomb to enshrine their memory. Benefactors of lesser fame may need their graven figures, their epitaphs of brass or alabaster; of Jocelin of Wells we may truly say—

"Si monumentum requiris, circumspice."

LECTURE III.

I HAVE in my former lectures carried the history both of the fabric and the foundation of the church of Wells to the time of Jocelin, and somewhat later. The thirteenth century, the great creative century of later English history, brought both fabric and foundation to a state, if not of ideal, at least of essential perfection. We now come to two centuries which found much to improve and to enlarge, but which had no need, like their predecessors, to begin afresh from the beginning. Jocelin, we may say, was the last of the line of great innovators for good and for evil, the line formed by Ine and Eadward and Gisa and John de Villulâ and Robert. We now come to what we may call quieter times. One thing to be noticed is that by this time the work of John de Villulâ, the degradation of Wells and exaltation of Bath, has been pretty well reversed. Roger, the successor of Jocelin, may be called the last Bath Bishop. In his election Bath made its last effort. On Jocelin's death the monks of Bath, contrary to the agreement which had been made, ventured to make an election without joining with the Canons of Wells. The story is very characteristic of the reign of Henry the Third. The Pope and the King joined together to do an illegal act to the prejudice of Englishmen. The monks of Bath got their *congé d'élire* from the King; then they elected in this irregular way; the elect went to the Pope, Innocent the Fourth, who, glad no doubt of such an opportunity, took no heed to the appeal of the Wells Chapter, conferred the Bishoprick on Roger by his own authority, bargaining that the preferment which he vacated, the Precentorship of Salisbury, should be given to his own nephew. The new Bishop was consecrated at Rome, and the temporalities were restored to him by the King.[1] This is a sort of thing which could hardly have happened at any time earlier or later. Both in earlier and in later times we suffered a good deal at the hands of both Kings and Popes, but Henry the Third was the only King who habitually conspired with the Pope against his own people. It really adds to the shamelessness of the whole story that, when Innocent had gained his personal point, when he had established the precedent that the Pope might if he pleased appoint to an English Bishoprick, when he had further established his own kinsman in an English living, he then was ready enough to confirm the former agreement, and to decree that the rights of the Chapter of Wells in the election of the Bishop should be observed for the future.[2] Roger also made up what he could to the Wells Chapter by the grant of various advantages.[3] He did not, however, think good to choose his last resting-place among them. He was the last of our Bishops who was buried at Bath. This marks the time when Wells once more became the real home of the Bishoprick, though Bath still retained its precedence in the episcopal title. And it was doubtless from this time that that comparative neglect of the church of Bath began which ended, as I have already said, in its falling into a state of decay verging on ruin.

During the time that followed I need not go through every Bishop in succession, as several Bishops seem to have had very little to do with the fabric. William Button the First, who was Bishop from 1247 to 1264, was chiefly remarkable for a practice which we certainly have not seen among us for some time past, but of which the traces still linger. In his day all the chief places of the church were filled with the Bishop's own kinsfolk. It was no doubt a most comfortable family party when the Bishop was surrounded by a Dean, Precentor, Treasurer, Archdeacon, and Provost, all of them his own brothers and nephews.(⁴) Yet mark that, though the fact of being the kinsman of a Bishop does not prove a man to be fit for high preferment, it does not prove him to be unfit. One of the Buttons, William the Second, first Archdeacon and afterwards Bishop from 1267 to 1274, was looked on as the holiest Prelate of his time, and after his death miracles were held to be worked at his tomb.(⁵) So they were said to be at the tomb of William of March, Bishop from 1293 to 1302.(⁶) Between these two saintly persons came Robert Burnell, whose place, whether in the history of England or in the history of Wells, is by no means small, but whose name is not specially connected with the fabric or foundation of the cathedral. In general history he appears as the minister of the great Edward; we know him here as the builder of that noble, but alas ruined, hall in the episcopal palace, which may take its place alongside of the great works of Gower at Saint David's.(⁷) For the next Bishop who claims any minute notice in a sketch of this kind we have to hurry on to the reign of Edward the Third, when a worthy successor of Robert and Jocelin meets us in the fortifier of the palace, the founder of the Vicars' Close, the famous Ralph of Shrewsbury.

Great works had been going on in the cathedral from the beginning of the century, although we do not find the name of any Bishop distinctly connected with them. The fact is that, now that the Chapters had gained so great a degree of corporate independence, the Bishops naturally become less prominent in such works than they were at an earlier time. The church, as designed by Jocelin, had hardly been brought to perfection by the building of the Chapter-house, when a series of works were begun which had the effect of completely transforming the whole eastern part of the church. There is reason to believe that the arrangements of the church of Jocelin were, like its style of architecture, a little old-fashioned. In the thirteenth century the tendency was to enlarge the eastern limbs of churches on a larger scale. The famous rebuilding of the choir of Canterbury late in the twelfth century had most likely set the example. The choir was now commonly placed in the eastern limb, which sometimes swelled to a length as great or greater than that of the nave. Sometimes the choir itself became cruciform by the addition of an eastern transept. Jocelin's church, on the other hand, still kept its choir under the tower, and east of the tower there was only a presbytery of three bays—the present choir—with some small chapels beyond it on the site of the present presbytery. The new scheme involved a complete recasting of all this part of the church, which seems to have been done from one general design which was carried out bit by bit. They began, as usual, at the east end, and with that part of the work which involved the least disturbance of the existing building. A distinct addition was made at the east end, an addition covering new ground which had not hitherto been part of the church. This addition was no other than the present beautiful Lady chapel, with the small transept immediately to the west of it. With the exquisite beauty of the Lady chapel every one is familiar; but every one may not have remarked how distinct it is from the rest of the church. Unlike any other of the component parts of the church, it could stand perfectly well by itself as a detached building. As it is, it gives an apsidal form to the extreme east end of the church; but it is much more than an apse; it is in fact an octagon no less than the Chapter-house, and to this form it owes much of its beauty. As an octagon standing detached at one end and joined to other buildings at the other end, it allowed the apsidal end to be combined with the exquisite slender shafts which open into the space to the west. But it must be remembered that the chapel must at first have stood almost as a detached building, and that, though it was doubtless not intended to remain so, yet the fact of its original isolation clearly had an effect on its form. There is a second transept at Wells, but, instead of dividing the choir from the presbytery, it is a mere appendage to the Lady chapel, and it is therefore far from being the important feature which the eastern transept is at Canterbury and Salisbury. The Lady chapel, with this dependent transept, clearly formed the first instalment of this general reconstruction of the eastern part of the church; and it appears, by an incidental notice in a document quoted by Professor Willis, that it was finished before the year 1326.(³) Then came the reconstruction of the eastern limb itself. This, as I said, involved an utter change in all the arrangements of the church. The eastern limb was to be lengthened by the addition of three bays, or, to speak more accurately, by substituting three bays of the full height of the church for whatever chapels had formerly stood on the site. These three bays were to form the presbytery, while the former presbytery was to be fitted up as the choir; that is to say, the stalls of the Canons were to be placed where they are now, instead of being under the tower. You must all have marked for yourselves the great difference in style between the three bays of Jocelin's work which now form the choir and the three added bays which now form the presbytery. They furnish a good study of the difference between the architecture of the thirteenth and the architecture of the fourteenth century. The two are put side by side, and their several details may be easily compared. And yet the contrast is perhaps not a perfectly fair one. The two pieces of work are rather extreme cases in opposite ways.

The earlier work retains something of the character of the style earlier still; as I have said all along, it is not typical English architecture of the thirteenth century, but has something of Romanesque leaven hanging to it. On the other hand, the new work, though exceedingly graceful, is perhaps rather too graceful; it has a refinement and minuteness of detail which is thoroughly in place in a small building like the Lady chapel, but which gives a sort of feeling of weakness when it is transferred to a principal part of the church of the full height of the building. The three elder arches are all masculine vigour; the three newer arches are all feminine elegance; but it strikes me that feminine elegance, thoroughly in its place in the small chapels, is hardly in its place in the presbytery. That the same style can be worked with great vigour and boldness is shown by the nave of York Minster. The next stage, after the addition of the new presbytery, would be the attempt to adapt what had now become the choir to the new work. You all know that Jocelin's triforium and clerestory have vanished, or nearly so, from the three bays of the choir, and that a clerestory and a triforium, if I may call it so, in the same style as the three new bays, have taken its place. I conceive that this work was not absolutely contemporary with the addition of the presbytery. If it had been done exactly at the same time, care would surely have been taken to keep the arcade, triforium, and clerestory exactly on the same level. There could be no motive for doing otherwise. I take the case to be this. The three bays were added, as such additions often were, without any regard to the style or proportion of the original building, beyond keeping the walls themselves at the same height. In an addition, like the presbytery, built in an utterly different style and without any adaptation to the earlier work, it was of no great moment whether the three divisions of the elevation exactly agreed or not with the levels of the older work. But a little later, probably when the roof came to be added, the idea suggested itself of bringing the three older bays into harmony, as far as might be, with the newer ones. The roofing of the presbytery would naturally suggest this change; it would perhaps make it absolutely necessary. For the form of roof chosen for the new work was of a kind very different from the older vaults of the church, and of a kind very singular and unusual. It is in fact a coved roof, such as we are used to in woodwork in this part of England, only with cells cut in it for the clerestory windows.(°) Such a roof could hardly have been added to the three eastern bays without disturbing the original roof of the three western bays; and it could hardly have been, as it was, carried over the three western bays also without disturbing the original triforium and clerestory. When therefore the design of the roof of the presbytery was determined on, the attempt was made to adapt the triforium and clerestory of the choir to those of the new work. But it was now impossible to keep the exact levels, and the result is what we see. You will remark that the upper stages of the choir were not, strictly speaking, rebuilt, but were simply cased and new windows inserted. The latter process, as is to be seen on the outside, was somewhat awkwardly done. The aisles of the choir were also recast at the same time by the addition of a vault and the insertion of windows in the new style.

The choir and presbytery, as we see them now, were thus finished in the course of the first half of the fourteenth century, but there may be some question as to the exact date. Professor Willis quotes an order of Chapter in 1325, by which each Canon was ordered to make his own stall at his own cost. The Professor infers that at that time the new choir was ready for the stalls to be placed in it.([10]) But perhaps the words need not absolutely bear that meaning; and one or two things seem to me to look the other way. First of all, the style of the presbytery seems to point to a time somewhat later in the century. The windows have fully advanced, and not very good, Flowing tracery, and in the east window there is a distinct approach to the Perpendicular lines of the next style. The other details too seem to belong to quite the later stage of what is called the Decorated style; they show decided signs of the near approach of the latest form of Gothic, our own local Perpendicular. Then again, our famous Bishop Ralph of Shrewsbury, who sat from 1329 to 1363, and of whom I shall have presently to speak more fully, was buried between the steps of the choir and the high altar, having seemingly a detached tomb in the middle of the presbytery.([11]) His tomb, which was fenced in by a grating, was afterwards moved to the north side of the presbytery, but, as Bishop Godwin says in his quaint fashion, it "lost his grates by the way."([12])

I

But the original place of Ralph's tomb was a place of special honour; it was the place of a founder; Ralph held the same place in the new choir which Jocelin had held in the old one. The inference seems irresistible, that Ralph stood to the new work in somewhat of the same relation in which Jocelin stood to the old; that he was in some sort its founder; that, at the very least, it was done during his episcopate. I confess that these two considerations seem to me to outweigh the presumption drawn from the order of Chapter about making the stalls, which, after all, might have been made as a precaution before the works in the choir were begun just as well as after they were ended. I believe therefore that the recasting of the eastern limb, the addition of the new presbytery, the change of the old presbytery into a choir, and the architectural changes following on the change of arrangement, belong mainly to the days of Ralph of Shrewsbury.

These changes, you will see, finished the ground-plan of the church itself as it now stands. The church itself has not been extended northwards, southwards, eastwards, or westwards, since the days of Bishop Ralph. Nor, on the other hand, has any part of the church itself been destroyed. Other buildings have been attached to it, and parts of the subordinate buildings have perished, but the ground covered by the church itself is exactly the same now as it was when Ralph was buried before the high altar. As a church then, as a building set apart for divine worship, Saint Andrew's was now quite perfect and needed neither addition nor change. Nave, choir, presbytery, chapels, and the one necessary adjunct of the Chapter-house, were all finished. But besides the completion of the ground-plan, there was another great work to be done before the building could be said to be finished as a work of architecture. Jocelin had not carried his three towers above the height of the roofs; they were mere stumps, and the effect must have been unfinished and unsightly. In the course of the fourteenth and fifteenth centuries this defect was supplied. Indeed, as far as the central tower is concerned, the defect had been supplied already. I have carried on the history of the changes which affected the ground-plan as a continuous narrative, but the raising of the central tower and its consequences belong to the same period. The raising of the tower seems to have formed part of the general plan of recasting the whole part of the church east of the crossing, and it may actually have been the first instalment of the work. I may here perhaps say a few words on the general subject of central towers. As the principal feature of churches of the highest class, the central tower is all but confined to England and Normandy; in other parts of France it is common enough, but, reversing our English rule, it is common in churches of a smaller class, but nearly unknown in the great cathedrals and abbeys. I ought perhaps to say that I am now speaking mainly of Gothic buildings, not of Romanesque. The truest way of putting the case would perhaps be that the central tower, the direct representative of the cupola, is a Romanesque feature, prevalent everywhere in Romanesque times, but which England and Normandy alone retained in large churches of later date. The question of central tower or no central tower resolves itself into this; which is the greater merit in a cathedral or other great church—the highest amount of internal majesty, or the highest perfection of external outline? England and Normandy decided for the external outline; the rest of Western Christendom decided for the internal effect. A great French church, Amiens, Beauvais, Chartres, Rheims, Saint Quentin, is carried up to a height in the inside of which we in England have no notion. But this internal majesty is bought by the utter sacrifice of external outline. The crossing of the four limbs of the church cries in vain for its natural crown in the central lantern. Indeed I am not clear that, if the central tower is left out, it is not better to leave out the transepts also. Certainly no churches ever impressed me more than those of Bourges and Alby, which follow this arrangement. Some of the great churches of France, which are most glorious within, are absolutely shapeless without. The central tower is impossible, and it is hard to adapt even western towers to a body of so great a height, unless their size is something prodigious. On the other hand, several of our English churches, on whose external outline the eye rests with the greatest pleasure, are positively depressing when we go in. Such above all is Lincoln; nothing can surpass the grouping of its three towers, but the effect of the lowness of the choir roof is positively crushing. The only church in England which affects great internal height is that of Westminster, and there, though a central tower was certainly designed, it seems to have been found impossible to carry it up.

The general look of Westminster Abbey is therefore much more that of a French than that of an English church. I know of one church only which thoroughly combines both kinds of merit, namely, the church of Saint Ouen at Rouen. There are French churches of greater height; there are English and Norman churches of more perfect outline. But no other church of equal internal height carries a central tower; no other church finished with a central tower can boast of the same internal height. Inferior to Amiens in one point, to Lincoln in another, I place Saint Ouen's, as a whole, above either.

Turn we now to our own church of Wells, a church, I need not say, built on a much smaller scale than any of those of which I have been speaking. It was of course designed, according to the usual English custom, for a central tower, though most likely Jocelin did not think of carrying it up so high as was afterwards done. This was constantly the case; a tower was carried up to a vast height, in what we cannot help calling a reckless way, on piers and arches which had been designed only for a much smaller weight. The natural consequence followed; the supports began to give way under the vast mass which was laid upon them, and, to keep the whole from falling, some means or other of propping, in a way necessarily more or less awkward, had to be resorted to. In many cases the tower actually fell down, as the spire of Chichester fell a few years ago. That it fell at that particular moment seems to have been pure matter of accident. It had always been dangerous; it might just as well have fallen three or four hundred years sooner, or it might just as well have lasted three or four hundred years longer. So at Salisbury, that lovely spire, so graceful to the sight, is constructively an excrescence which ought never to have been placed there, which the piers below it were never designed to support, and which has been kept up to this day only by using various props and devices from time to time. Our own case at Wells was bad enough, though not nearly so bad as at Chichester and Salisbury. The tower was carried up between the years 1318 and 1321,([13]) but if any spire was ever added or designed, it was simply one of wood and lead, like those which have vanished from all the three towers of Lincoln. Hence, though the weight which was laid on the piers was much greater than they were able to bear, it was not so great as at Salisbury and Chichester, and the danger and destruction has not been so great as it has been in those two cases. The tower then was raised, and the usual results followed, results which have been graphically described by Professor Willis both at Wells and in other places. The increased height caused the four great piers to sink into the ground. This of course tore away the masonry of the four limbs of the church from their connexion with the piers; the new tower, perhaps as yet hardly brought to perfection, stood, so to speak, on four lame legs, on four supports which were giving way beneath it, and yawning gaps began to appear between the tower arches and the main walls of the church. Thus, within twenty years after its first building, in the years 1337 and 1338,([14]) the tower needed to be strengthened by supports which the first builders had never thought of, and the damage which had already been actually done had to be made good. The tower at Wells had to be propped like the towers at Canterbury and Salisbury. The question at once follows as to the way in which the propping was done. Any support of the kind must be more or less unsightly; thrust in as an afterthought, to remedy a constructive defect, it cannot fail to interfere with the original design and the original proportions. No one would have put them there, if he could have helped it; if constructive reasons had not called for the props, they would have been better away. When we compare the way in which this needful, though unpleasant, work was done in the different cases, we shall see a kind of clumsy ingenuity about the Wells work which may call for a certain measure of praise. At Salisbury and Canterbury the prop takes the form of a horizontal screen running across the arches. Such a form is more elegant in itself, and it interferes less with the general appearance of the building. But it is more distinctly an excrescence; it forces itself more strongly on the eye as something stuck in than when the props are worked into the earlier work in the way that they are at Wells. You all know the low arches under the lantern with the inverted arches on the top of them, the great circles in the spandrils, the whole arch turned into a kind of pattern of gigantic Geometrical tracery. It is very heavy, very clumsy; till the eye gets thoroughly familiar with it, it seems very ugly; but it is in every way ingenious. The prop is worked and fitted into the old work in a way in which it is not in the other cases. I can even think it possible that people who do not know the history, and who do not at once see from its details that it is an insertion, may even mistake it for part of the original design. And, granting its position at all, granting the peculiar form which it takes, there is something in the detail or rather lack of detail, something in the great size of the few mouldings and the absence of capitals and shafts, which seems to suit the boldness of the general outline. And I am not sure whether there is not a further propriety in the form chosen. The lines of the inverted arches roughly suggest a Saint Andrew's cross, and it may be that we have here, now that the affairs of Wells were beginning to brighten, a new trophy of success offered to the now triumphant elder brother.([15])

The object of the inverted arches was strictly to support the tower by strengthening its piers. Other changes were needed to make good the damage done by the tearing away of the masonry on each side. This involved a partial blocking of the clerestory and triforium in the bays adjoining the tower, so as to make a set of gigantic flying-buttresses for its support. The pier-arches below them had most likely been quite shattered; those at least in the nave and transept certainly had been. New arches in the style of the fourteenth century were accordingly inserted, and it is instructive at once to compare the difference of their details from those of the original work, and to trace the exact extent of the new masonry. As ever, the mediæval builders wasted nothing; every stone of the old work which could be kept in its place or used again they did keep in its place or use again. And though the details are of exactly the same date and style as those of the inverted arches, it is worth while to notice the extreme boldness with which the mouldings are wrought in the great arches, and the extreme delicacy with which they are wrought in the smaller ones. Altogether it is plain that the raising of the tower must have been done recklessly and without due regard to the strength of its supports. It is plain also that the result of this reckless building has been the lasting disfigurement of the church by the insertion of props which the eye wishes away. Still, as the disfigurement had to be made, we must allow the praise of considerable ingenuity to the way in which it was made.

All that was now lacking to the fabric of the church was the completion of the western towers. The general effect of these towers is so exactly alike that no one would guess that nearly fifty years passed between the building of the two. A minute examination will reveal certain small differences. The height of the two towers is not exactly the same, and a niche which is found on one is not repeated on the other. But these are not differences of style: they are just the same kind of differences as those which we find at an earlier time between the different parts of the nave. Still it is strange to find that a gap of so many years had made absolutely no difference at all in style strictly so called. But this, at this time at least, is characteristic of the district. The Perpendicular style was introduced into Somersetshire very early, and it remained in use for a long time without any material change. Between the earliest and the latest examples there undoubtedly is a difference, but it is a difference much slighter than is usual in other parts of the country. In many cases there is no perceptible difference of style between buildings separated by an interval of a good many years. I have therefore always declined to guess at the dates of Perpendicular buildings in Somersetshire, when no documentary evidence could be brought forward; and I think that the case of the western towers of Wells shows that I have been discreet in so doing. I do not think that any one would have found out the difference in date between these towers by simply looking at them, and I think that any one would have been inclined, from simply looking at them, to place the earlier of the two a good deal later than its real date. I must confess that, knowing as I do that they are nearly fifty years apart, I sometimes find it hard to remember whether it is the northern or the southern tower which is the older. In fact, the southern one is the older. It was built in the time of John Harewell, who was Bishop from 1366 to 1386, at the joint cost of himself and the Chapter, the Chapter paying two-thirds and the Bishop one.([16]) The tower therefore belongs to the very first days of the Perpendicular style; it must have followed so soon upon the east window of the choir, that we may count the completion of the western towers as really parts of the same work as the changes in the eastern part of the church. The other, the northern tower, was built in the days, and largely at the cost, of Bishop Bubwith,([17]) whose name is well known to us all by reason of his hospital and his chantry chapel. He has also a special place in the municipal history of the city, through his gift of the old Guildhall to the citizens. His episcopate lasted from 1408 to 1424, so that the very considerable difference of date between the building of the two towers is clearly marked.

Nothing more remains to be spoken of in the fabric of the church itself, beyond a few insertions in the Perpendicular style—such, for instance, as the window tracery inserted in the nave and transept. I do not know the exact date of this not very important change, but it must have been late in the fourteenth or early in the fifteenth century. For it is plain that it was made before the reconstruction of the cloister and the addition of the rooms over it, as these last block one of the windows inserted in the transept. Now these rooms were built by Bishop Bubwith,[b] so that the insertion of the tracery was made before his time, not improbably when the southern tower was carried up. A more important change, and one which must have happened later, was the insertion of a fan-tracery vault in the central tower, hiding the original arcades which remain above it. One hardly sees the reason of this insertion, as there could be no reason for hanging bells in the central tower of a church which had two towers at the west end.

Thus, after about two hundred years from the beginning of the present building in the days of Jocelin, we may look on the cathedral church of Saint Andrew as at last finished. It was finished, in a sense, before the end of the thirteenth century, when everything had been built which was needed for its ecclesiastical completeness. But it was in the course of the fifteenth century that it finally assumed the shape with which we are all familiar, and which has from that time remained almost unchanged. Now then we have reached the point at which we can estimate the place which fairly belongs to the church of Wells among the other churches of England and of Christendom. As it seems to me, that position, as I began by saying, is a special and remarkable one. I need not say that, in point of size and splendour, the church of Wells has no claim to a place in the first rank of European, or even of English, churches. Setting aside the Welsh churches, and the churches which have become cathedral without being originally meant for that rank, Wells is one of the very smallest of English episcopal churches. It is hardly fair to compare it with Carlisle, which is a mere fragment, or with Hereford, which has lost its western tower, and with it a part of its nave. But it is, in point of scale, with Carlisle, Hereford, Lichfield, and Rochester, or again with non-cathedral churches like Southwell, Beverley, and Tewkesbury, that Wells must fairly be compared, not with churches like Canterbury and York, or even like Salisbury and Gloucester. And among churches of its own class it certainly ranks very high. It has one accidental advantage in having been much less damaged by mere destroyers than any of them, except perhaps Beverley. But this is not all. I think that those under whose hands the church of Wells gradually grew up showed a wiser discretion, and a greater skill in adapting their changes and additions to what they found existing, than was shown in most of the other cases. Let us take the two ends of the church, the two parts to which a church owes so much of its external character, the east end and the west front. Now the west front of Wells is a thing which it is the fashion to rave about. It is the finest part of the church; the finest thing in Somersetshire; the finest thing in England; for aught I know, the finest thing in the world. I am perverse enough to think differently, and to look on the west front as the one part of the church of Wells which is thoroughly bad in principle. It is doubtless the finest display of sculpture in England; but it is thoroughly bad as a piece of architecture. I am always glad when I get round the corner, and can rest my eye on the massive and simple majesty of the nave and transepts. The west front is bad, because it is a sham—because it is not the real ending of the nave and aisles, but a mere mask, devised in order to gain greater room for the display of statues. The architecture, in short, is sacrificed to the sculpture. A real honest west front, if it have two towers, will be made by the real gable of the nave flanked by a tower at the end of each aisle. So it is at York; so it is at Abbeville; so it is at Llandaff. Or a front may, like those of Winchester, Gloucester, and Bath, have no towers at all, but may simply consist of the endings of the nave and aisles, set off with turrets and pinnacles. Or a front may be, like that one glorious and unequalled front at Peterborough, built up in front of and across the endings of the nave and aisles, but without at all professing to be itself their finish. All these forms are honest; but I deny the honesty of such fronts as those at Wells, Salisbury, and Lincoln.([19]) In all these cases the front is not the natural finish of the nave and aisles; it is a blank wall built up in a shape which is not the shape which their endings would naturally assume. It is therefore a sham; it is a sin against the first law of architectural design, the law that enrichment should be sought in ornamenting the construction, in giving a pleasing form, and such enrichment as may be thought good, to those features which the construction makes absolutely necessary, not in building up anything simply for the sake of effect. The main features in a front should be the windows and doorways. There must be some windows and some doorways; it is the business of the architect to make these necessary features the main sources of ornament. Now in the Wells front the windows and doorways are made nothing of; they could not be altogether got rid of, but they seem to have been felt as mere interruptions to the lines of sculpture. They are therefore stowed away as they best may be, and they do not form, as they should, the main features of the front. Look, for instance, at Llandaff; the front suffers much from the incongruity of the two towers built at different times: but look at the ending of the nave itself; that perfect composition of lancets, inside and out, is, as it should be, the main feature; at Wells the west window is made nothing of; it is simply cut through the sculpture. The small size of doorways is a common fault of English as opposed to foreign churches; but at Wells they reach the extreme point of insignificance in those narrow mouse-holes at the end of the aisles, through one of which we are commonly driven to creep, while the west doorway remains shut. But even the west doorway itself is a very small mouthful, I will not say after Laon or Rheims, but after York; nay even at Lichfield and Salisbury the doorways have a little more of dignity than they have at Wells. In a really good design the architectural features ought to be the first thing; sculpture or any other source of ornament should be secondary. At Wells the rule is reversed; a sham wall is built up and loaded with statues, and the windows and doorways are left to shift for themselves.

You may perhaps be surprised, perhaps even a little indignant, at the freedom of my criticism on a work which you have doubtless all learned to look on with traditional admiration. But there is nothing like truth, and I think that, if you go and fairly examine for yourselves, you will see that the censures which I have made on our west front rest on good grounds. Those censures are pretty well summed up in the one charge of unreality. But, if we can get over that charge, there is much to be said for the design on the score of boldness and originality. You know that the towers, instead of standing, as usual, at the ends of the aisles, stand beyond them, an arrangement which I have seen nowhere else except in the metropolitan church of Rouen.([20]) Now in a church of the comparatively small size of Wells the effect of this arrangement is undoubtedly to sacrifice height to width, and thereby to take away from the truest dignity of the front. Still it is not to be denied that even the width has a dignity of its own, and the arrangement was well planned with regard to the special object in view, that of gaining the greatest possible space for the display of sculpture. And after all, though the west front of Wells is a sham, it is by no means so contemptible a sham as the west fronts of either Salisbury or Lincoln. The form given to the front, if unreal, is at least stately. At Salisbury the form given to the front is equally unreal, and it is indescribably mean; as no western towers were intended, one cannot conceive why the natural endings of the nave and aisles were not left, as at Winchester, Gloucester, and Bath, and in our great parish churches of Yatton and Crewkerne. The Wells front again is at least a whole; the Lincoln front is a mass of incongruous pieces. Large parts of two earlier fronts are left to disturb the harmony of the design, and a blank wall is actually carried in front of two of the noblest towers in the world, as if of set purpose to destroy their effect. The Wells front, after all, unreal as it is, has more connexion with the main building than that of Beverley, where a front, poorly imitated from that of York, is built up against the church, with a gable which has no reference whatever to the real gable of the nave.([21]) At Wells, again the later builders seem to have had more feeling than usual for the harmony of the front. Wells has not suffered like Southwell, where a huge Perpendicular window was cut through the noble Romanesque front, and a sham wall with a flat battlement carried up above it. The towers were carried up in the fourteenth and fifteenth centuries in a way which harmonizes very well with the general design of the front, though there is no kind of adaptation to its details. And here comes the question which I believe everybody asks at a first sight of Wells

Cathedral. As I once heard it clearly and tersely put, " Well, that is a fine piece of work, but what are those pieces without their tops ? " Every one, I suppose, feels the unfinished look of the towers; the eye craves for something or other more than there is, be it pinnacles, spires, or anything else. Now I once very carefully examined the tops of the towers in company with Mr. Parker, and we could see no signs that there ever had been, or had been designed to be, any stone-work more than there is now. But any sort of finish that any one chooses to imagine may have been added, or designed to be added, in wood. I suspect that people seldom take in how many of our great churches had their towers finished with spires of wood covered with lead or shingle. Spires of this sort were either destroyed by accident or taken away in wantonness at Old Saint Paul's, Lincoln, Ely, Hereford, Exeter, Southwell, and a crowd of other churches. A single one of two still remains at Ottery Saint Mary. On the Continent they are far more common, and they sometimes furnish beautiful examples of work in lead. Among the English examples, the towers of Lincoln supply the example which is most instructive for our own case. The spires are gone, but the angle turrets are still finished with pinnacles of wood covered with lead. Whether such an arrangement as this ever actually existed at Wells I do not know, but there can be no doubt that a finish of this kind, spires of wood sheeted with lead, with pinnacles of the same materials at the angles, would be the true means of getting rid of the flat and imperfect look of which every one complains.

K

If we turn to the east end, we shall, as I have already said, find the church of Wells holding a far higher position among its fellows. The east ends of English churches are of various kinds; the apsidal form, that most usual on the Continent, being the rarest. We do indeed find the German apse without aisles repeated at Lichfield, and the French apse with its divergent chapels is found on a vast scale at Westminster, and on a smaller at Tewkesbury. And there are a few other examples of apses of less merit and importance at Pershore, Coventry, Wrexham, and a few other places.([22]) But the apsidal arrangement never was thoroughly English. Of the three great examples Tewkesbury is the only one where the apse fills its proper function of a canopy over the high altar. At Westminster the high altar is displaced by the shrine of Eadward the Confessor, and at Lichfield it is not the choir, but a Lady chapel of the full height, of which the apse is the ending. English east ends fall for the most part under two classes. Sometimes, as at York, Lincoln, Ely, Beverley, and Southwell, the Lady chapel and whatever else stands east of the high altar is carried on at the full height of the church. In other cases, as at Winchester, Hereford, Exeter, and Salisbury, the Lady chapel and other chapels east of the choir are much lower than the main body of the church. Now of these arrangements I confess that I myself prefer the apse to all others. No other plan gives such dignity to the high altar, or makes it so evidently the central and crowning point of the whole church. There is undoubtedly great stateliness in such an arrangement as that of York and Lincoln; but its good effect is almost wholly confined to the outside. The high altar seems to have come where it is by accident; its position is marked by a mere screen, not by anything in the arrangement of the building itself. In the third arrangement, where all that is east of the choir is much lower than the choir, some share of its proper dignity is or may be restored to the high altar. But, on the other hand, it is not easy to add on a lower building which shall be in full harmony with the loftier parts of the church. There is something insignificant about the Lady chapel at Salisbury, and it is hard to admire, externally at least, the long masses of low chapels at Winchester and Saint Alban's. A happy accident, as I have already explained, gave the opportunity at Wells of producing a form of east end which I think certainly surpasses all others of its class. The general outline and proportion of the church are no less excellent, and it is fortunate in having had everything finished, and in having nothing destroyed. At Hereford, as I have already said, the western tower has vanished, and it has carried part of the nave away with it. But, even while it stood, the single western tower could never have grouped so well with the central lantern as the two western towers at Wells. Wimborne, the chief surviving example of this arrangement, I have heard irreverently compared to driving tandem, and I cannot deny the aptness of the saying.[25] At Southwell, where the grouping of the three towers is as perfect as it well may be, the general effect has greatly suffered by the lowering of the roofs throughout. We shall hardly venture to compare the four limbs of Wells with the four limbs of Beverley, but of the Beverley west front I have already spoken, and the general effect of the church is altogether ruined through the central tower never having been carried up. Even at Lichfield, the faultless grace of the three spires, even the loveliness of the apse, cannot reconcile us to the long low body and to the extravagant length of the eastern limb. The eastern view of Lichfield, graceful as it is, cannot compare with the real stateliness of the east end of Wells. I have seen many fine churches both in our own country and abroad, many of them of course on a scale which might seem to put Wells out of all comparison. But I can honestly say that I know of no architectural group which surpasses the harmony and variety of our own cathedral, as seen by the traveller as he first enters the city from Shepton Mallet.

From the outside we turn to that of which the outside is after all the mere shell. When we enter the church, we find ourselves in a building which can fairly hold its own against competitors of its own class. The nave has a distinct character of its own: there may be differences of taste as to its merit, but it has a character, and that character is clearly the result of design. The main lines of the interior are horizontal rather than vertical. We can hardly say that there is any division into bays; no vaulting-shafts run up from the ground, nor does the triforium take, as usual, the form of a distinct composition over each arch. In short we cannot, as we can in most churches, take each arch with the triforium and clerestory over it as a thing existing by itself. One would rather say that three horizontal ranges, one over the other, all converged to the centre, without thinking of what was above or below them. Now tastes may differ as to whether this is a good arrangement or not, but there is no doubt that it is in its way an effective arrangement; there is no nave in which the eye is so irresistibly carried eastward as in that of Wells. And it is worth notice that this arrangement, in its fulness, is confined to the nave; in the transepts the bays are much more clearly marked. The idea of producing this marked horizontal effect was clearly one which came into the heads of the designers as they were working westwards.

It might have been expected that the marked prominence which is thus given to the horizontal line might have gone far to destroy all effect of height in the interior; but it is not so. There is no special feeling of height in Wells Cathedral—not so much, for instance, as there is in the church of Saint Mary Redcliff; but there is no such crushing feeling of lowness as there is at Lincoln. This I imagine to be mainly owing to the form of the arch chosen for the vaulting, one boldly but not acutely pointed, and to the way in which the lantern-arches fit into the vault. Contrast this with the far larger and loftier nave of York. In that nave the positive height is second only to Westminster among English churches, and the design of the separate bays can hardly be surpassed in its soaring effect. But in the direct eastern or western view the nave of York loses almost its whole effect, partly, no doubt, from the excessive breadth, but partly also from the flat and crushing shape of the vaulting-arch. Another point which I think helps to redress the balance between horizontal and vertical effect is the great height of the clerestory. In a church where the vertical bays are strongly marked I do not think that great comparative height in the clerestory helps to increase the effect of height. But in such cases the question rather lies between the arcade as one thing, and the triforium and clerestory together as another. Here the question lay between the triforium and the clerestory, and I cannot help thinking that, if the triforium had been on the same scale as that in the choir of Ely, the effect of height would have been less. At any rate, the nave of Wells makes the most of its small actual height: so do the choir and presbytery also; for, though I cannot at all admire the kind of vault which is there used, the shape of the arch is as judiciously chosen as it is in the nave. In the presbytery we also get the vaulting-shafts rising from the ground, so as to give the vertical division, and the consequent effect of height, in its highest perfection. Of the exquisite beauty of the Lady chapel, looked on, as it should be, not as a part of the whole, but as a distinct and almost detached building, I have already spoken. In short, the internal effect of the church, whether looked at as a whole or taken in its several parts, if not of the highest order, which its comparatively small scale forbids, may claim a high place among churches of its own class.

I think then on the whole that, even looking at the church by itself, we have every reason to be thankful for what we have got. We have not a church of the first order; but we have a church whose several parts fit very well together, all whose parts have been finished, and of which no part has been destroyed. And I may add that we may be thankful for another thing, for the goodness of the stone of which the greater part of the church is built. The sculpture of the west front indeed has crumbled away; but elsewhere at Wells, as at Glastonbury, wherever the work has not been wantonly knocked away, it is as good as when it was first cut. Now we might have had a church like Chester or Coventry, where the whole surface of the stone has crumbled away, and where the whole ornamental design has become unintelligible. I have said that the church of Wells forms a harmonious whole, that it was perfectly finished, and that no part has been destroyed; and this is a great thing to say. Let me compare the good fortune of Wells in this respect with the cathedral church of a much more famous city at the other end of England. At Carlisle there is a noble choir, ending in what is probably the grandest window in England. If that choir only had transepts, nave, and towers to match it, the church of Carlisle would be a splendid church indeed. But the choir is built up against a little paltry transept and central tower, and nothing remains by way of nave but two bays of the original small Norman church, the rest having utterly vanished. Here then is a church which does not form a harmonious whole, a church which remains utterly unfinished, and of which one essential part has been destroyed. Or, without taking such an extreme case as this, we may compare our church with some of those of which I have already spoken, with Hereford, Southwell, Beverley, and Tewkesbury. In all of these some important feature has either never been finished or has been destroyed at a later time. The church of Wells then, simply taken by itself, claims a high place among buildings of its own class, that is, among minsters of the second order. But, as I began these lectures by saying, the real charm of Wells does not lie in the church taken by itself, but in the church surrounded by its accompanying buildings. Of some of these I must now speak a word. I do not intend to go minutely into either their architecture or their history; but some of them are inseparably connected both with the fabric and with the foundation of the cathedral. And it is the preservation of them which gives Wells its peculiar character. Each part may easily be equalled or surpassed, but the whole has no rival in England, and I cannot think that it has many in Christendom.

It was during the fourteenth and fifteenth centuries, alongside of the works in the church itself of which I have already spoken, that those subordinate buildings were also rising, which have given Wells this its peculiar character as the most complete and most uninjured example of the buildings of a great secular foundation. The greatest name in this way in the course of the fourteenth century is one which we all know, that of Bishop Ralph of Shrewsbury; I have already spoken of him as having probably had a chief hand in the reconstruction of the choir and presbytery. He also gave the palace its present form. The house had been originally built by Jocelin. The great hall had been added by Robert Burnell. It was Ralph who fenced himself in with a moat and a wall as we now see.([24]) But his greatest work is to be looked for on the other side of the church, and it is closely connected with the constitutional change which may be looked on as putting the finishing stroke to the existing constitution of the cathedral, I mean the foundation of the College of Vicars. The great offices of the church were now all in being, and the relations between the two classes of Canons had been pretty well fixed. It now remained to fix the exact position of that subordinate body of clergy which had grown up through the prevalent practice of non-residence among the Canons. The Vicar, we have seen, was at first simply the personal deputy of some particular Canon, appointed by him to discharge his duties in his absence. But it could hardly fail that the Vicars as a body should gradually enter into some sort of relation with the Chapter as a body. This would especially be the case, when residence became the fixed duty of one class of Canons and no part of the duty of another. The Vicars would gradually change from deputies of absent Canons into assistants of Canons who at least professed to be present. As such, it was natural that they should receive a fixed status in the church, and, with the ideas of those times, it was equally natural that they should receive somewhat of corporate independence. The Vicars of Wells then, like the Vicars of most or all of the Old Foundation churches, became a distinct corporation. They were subordinate to the Chapter as regards their duties in the church, but they were independent of it as regards the estates with which they were endowed, and they were governed by statutes given them by their founder. That founder was, as we all know, Ralph of Shrewsbury. Most of you, no doubt, have seen the picture with the Latin verses in which the Vicars set forth their hard case to the Bishop, how they are driven to live where they can about the town, and how he promises to give them a house where they may live together.([25]) Then arose the Vicars' Close of Wells, and, though the present buildings mainly belong to a later time, yet portions of Ralph's work may still be seen, especially in the hall, where several of his windows still remain. But the complaint of the Vicars, that they were scattered through the streets of the town, deserves notice. In the first state of things, as is plain from the stories told by Richard of the Devizes, the Vicar lived in the house of the Canon whom he represented.([26]) But it is equally plain that as the number of prebends increased, even the institution of ribs did not provide a house for every Canon, and, as the institution of special Residentiaries became fixed, the available houses would be mainly occupied by them. We can thus understand how there might now be many Vicars unprovided with any place to dwell in. The buildings of the Close were recast and almost rebuilt by the three executors of Bishop Beckington, Richard Swan the Provost, Hugh Sugar the Treasurer, and John Pope, Prebendary of Saint Decumans.([27]) They were commissioned to dispose of the unbequeathed portion of the Bishop's goods to pious uses at their discretion, and, besides other works in other parts of the diocese, the Vicars' Close now assumed its present shape. In that shape it is certainly without a rival. I know nothing to compare to those two quiet ranges of houses, the hall at one end, the chapel at the other, suggesting the very perfection of collegiate life; and, as an ingenious device for turning a piece of practical convenience into a matter of high architectural ornament, nothing can well surpass the chain-bridge. I need not say that the original design of the institution was at once broken in upon as soon as marriage was allowed to its members. The two rooms, with the separate approach to each, were designed as college rooms for men who took their meals in the common hall; and, as college rooms, they give very far from contemptible accommodation. But they were, of course, utterly unsuited for the reception of wives and families, and the architectural features of the Close have been sadly damaged by throwing two or more houses into one. I have always cherished a sort of dream that, by some means or other, the old institution of the Vicars' College and the new institution of the Theological College might be rolled into one, that the office of Vicar in the cathedral might be held by young clergymen and by men preparing for holy orders, and that collegiate life might be again restored in the old hall of Ralph and Beckington. But, however this may be, I would at least call on the clerical members of the College to stick to their good old title of Priest Vicar, and not to call themselves, or allow themselves to be called, by the new-fangled name of Minor Canon. It is historically incorrect; it was in use at Saint Paul's and at Hereford, but it was never in use at Wells. That it is better sounding or more honourable than that of Priest Vicar I cannot believe. To me it seems exactly the reverse, as the stress is always laid on the word *Minor*, never on the word *Canon*. And it tends to confound the Priest Vicars of our Old Foundations with men holding a position very inferior to theirs, namely the Petty Canons or Minor Canons of the churches founded by Henry the Eighth. These are simple subordinates of the Chapter, without any separate endowment or corporate independence of any kind. The supposed legal necessity for the change arises from a misconstruction of an Act of Parliament, which really orders nothing of the kind. To hear of a Minor Canon of Wells is as bad as to hear of an Honorary Canon; that is to say, to hear a Canon or Prebendary of Wells, whose stall dates perhaps from the twelfth century, pulled down to the level of those mysterious personages, not only without revenues but without either rights or duties, who have sprung up at Bristol or Manchester within the present reign.

The history of Vicars' Colleges at Wells and elsewhere should be written in full. No one could do it so well as my friend Mr. Dimock, once himself a Priest Vicar of the collegiate church of Southwell.([28]) One point to be worked out with special care would be the steps and causes by which the office came to be held by laymen. The change in this respect was fully recognized by the charter of Elizabeth, which confirmed the rights and estates of the Vicars, and regulated, without absolutely fixing, the numbers of the two classes of Vicars, clerical and lay. It is a change which has not taken place everywhere. The Vicars at York are still a purely clerical body, the lay members of the choir being mere stipendiaries. And, unless some change has been made very lately, the same is the case at Hereford.([29]) And as the Priest Vicars of our Old Foundations should never be confounded with the Petty Canons of the New, still less should the lay members of those colleges, equal in corporate rights to their clerical brethren, ever be degraded to the level of the mere lay clerks or singing-men of other churches, who are sometimes simply stipendiaries, and who, even when they are statutable officers, have no separate endowment or corporate being.

There were thus, before the end of the fourteenth century, two distinct corporations attached to the cathedral church, namely, the Chapter and the College of Vicars. These two were and are distinct and independent as regards their property and personal being, though, as regards the duty and discipline of the church, the members of the younger foundation were and are subordinate to the members of the elder. These two bodies still remain, and I trust they may long remain and flourish; but, in the first years of the fifteenth century, a third body arose, which has vanished from among us. We read that Ralph Erghum, who was Bishop from 1388 to 1401, and who was a benefactor to his church in several ways,([30]) founded by his will a College of fourteen priests in a place which was then called the *Mounterye*, and which from this foundation took the name of College Lane.(³¹) That is to say, he seems to have incorporated the Chantry-priests of the cathedral, the priests who, besides the public services performed by the Canons and Vicars, said masses for particular persons at particular altars. All foundations of this kind were suppressed by the Act of the first year of Edward the Sixth, and the only memory which Erghum's foundation has left among us is the name which still belongs to the lane.

The separate houses of Canons and other officers belong mainly to the fifteenth century, though there are some portions of earlier date. Let me here especially mention one small and decaying but very beautiful fragment, namely the round window with wooden tracery at the east end of the house which formerly belonged to the Archdeacons of Wells. The house itself, strangely disguised as it is without, contains within a very fine timber roof; the Deanery too, much as it has suffered from the insertion of modern windows, still retains much of the dignity of design which it received from its builder, the learned Dean Gunthorpe, who held the office from 1473 to 1498.(³²) But I will not enlarge more fully on the particular houses; they are the especial province of Mr. Parker, and he has dealt with them all from the Bishop's palace to the house of the organist.(³³) I would only again insist on the necessity, on the duty, of carefully preserving every one of these ancient buildings to the assemblage of which our city owes its special position among the cities of England. We have lost too much already. Every year some ancient building is destroyed or threatened.([34]) Let those whose business it is awake before it is too late; let them see that not another stone is sacrificed to niggardliness, to caprice, or to ignorant notions of improvement. Look, for instance, at what was some time back trumpeted as a vast improvement, the pulling down of a house to open a view of the west front of the Cathedral to the windows of the Swan Inn. The doers of that deed most likely knew not what they were doing. They perhaps did not even remember that, in opening the view of the west front of the Cathedral to the windows of the Swan Inn, they were also opening the not very picturesque view of the Swan Inn to those who came out of the western doors of the Cathedral. They did not stop to think that the space before the west front was really too open already, and that at any rate matters were not mended by opening a view through so ludicrous a gap, which I have heard witty people compare to the space left in a man's mouth by drawing a single tooth. Still less did they think that, in a thoughtless moment of destruction, they were wiping out the whole history of the church and city. The house indeed was in itself valueless; I should not have wept for the removal of the house or of the whole row of houses of which it formed a part. But, along with the house, the destroyers overthrew the wall against which the house was built up, and that wall was the history of the city of Wells. At Wells, as I have already set forth, the church was not founded in the city, but the city grew up under the shadow of the church.([35]) The church and its precincts were not taken into the city till the days of parliamentary and municipal reform. The wall of the Close is everywhere a sign of separation, marking off ecclesiastical and temporal property, and often marking the limits of distinct jurisdictions. But at Wells the wall has a special significance, as a memorial of the days when the city arose outside the ecclesiastical precinct. Thus, by a single thoughtless act, not only is a material piece of antiquity destroyed, but a page of local, and thereby of national, history is torn away.

The only remaining work to be mentioned is one to which I have incidentally referred more than once, namely, the cloister and the buildings attached to it. I have now to add that the detached Lady chapel in the east walk of the cloister was rebuilt by Robert Stillington, who was Bishop from 1464 to 1487, an event which is best recorded in the words of Bishop Godwin.

"He built that goodly Lady Chappell in the cloysters, that was pulled down by him that destroyed also the great hall of the palace . . . and was entombed in the said Chappell, but rested not long there: For it is reported, that divers olde men, who in their youth had not onely seene the celebration of his funerals, but also the building of his toombe, Chappell and all; did also see, toombe and Chappell destroyed, and the bones of the Bishop that built them, turned out of the lead in which they were interred."[36]

This quotation may serve as a fitting transition to the times which we have now reached. We have now done with the age of building up, and we have come to the age of pulling down. At the end of the fifteenth century the church of Wells had reached its highest degree of perfection. The church was complete; its appurtenances were complete. Of the fabric itself it is enough to say that our great Beckington, so bountiful a benefactor to the city and diocese in every other way, did nothing to the actual fabric of the cathedral, because there was really nothing for him to do. My subject, you will remember, is the cathedral church, alike in its fabric and in its constitution. Had my subject been the city generally, I should have found something to say about the parish church, about the hospitals, about the Guild-hall, about Beckington's houses in the marketplace. But I keep myself to the cathedral and its immediate belongings. The destruction spoken of in the extract which I just before made from Godwin carries us on to the reign of Edward the Sixth. But I must first say a few words about the reign of Henry the Eighth. I must now once more call on you carefully to bear in mind the distinction between the regular and secular clergy, and between the cathedral churches served by each of them severally. In the course of the reign of Henry the Eighth all the monastic foundations in England were destroyed. Everybody knows this fact, but everybody does not put the fact in its right place. People talk of an event called the Reformation, as if it were a single event which happened in some one particular year, like the passing of the Reform Bill or the cutting off of Charles the First's head. No such event ever happened. A great many ecclesiastical changes took place in the course of the sixteenth century, but those changes did not happen all at once, and many of them had no immediate connexion with one another. Above all, do not fancy that an old Church was destroyed and a new Church founded; do not fancy that property was taken from one set of clergy and given to another set of clergy. Nothing of the sort ever happened. Great changes were made *in* the Church of England, changes which, as some people at the time thought, went too far, and which, as other people thought, did not go far enough. But these changes in no way touched what we may call the personal identity of the Church before and after them. Remember that I am not talking theology but history. No one here will suppose that I, of all men, deny the power of Parliament to disestablish and disendow a Church, if it sees good reason to do so; I only say that, as a matter of fact, that power was not exercised by Parliament in the sixteenth century. Certain ecclesiastical changes were made; certain ecclesiastical foundations were suppressed; but the Church itself went on. The throwing off of the authority of the Bishop of Rome, the suppression of the monasteries, the introduction of the English Prayer-Book and Articles, were three different events, which happened at three different times, and which had nothing directly to do with one another. The monastic foundations accepted the King's supremacy just as fully as the secular foundations did, and, after the monasteries were suppressed, mass went on being said in the cathedral, collegiate, and parochial churches, just as it had been before. And let no one fancy that the two suppressions familiar to us in the reign of Henry the Eighth, the suppression of the lesser and of the greater monasteries, were the first cases of the suppression of ecclesiastical foundations known in England. The supreme power of the state in England has in all ages, as it has done in our own day, exercised that authority over the temporalities of the Church, which, in its own nature, it must exercise over everything. Cardinal Wolsey suppressed a number of small monasteries in order to transfer their endowments to his colleges at Ipswich and Oxford.([37]) Before that, in the reign of Henry the Fifth, the Alien Priories, that is the monasteries which were dependent on monasteries in foreign countries, were suppressed by Act of Parliament.([38]) The main difference is that in these cases monasteries were suppressed for good political reasons, and their revenues were applied to useful public purposes, while in the suppression under Henry and Cromwell all that was thought of was the scramble of the King and his courtiers for their own private pelf.([39]) The most sickening havoc and sacrilege ran wild among the noblest and holiest fabrics of the land. We have but to go as far as Glastonbury, to see the desolation of the most venerable spot in Britain, to ask in vain for the burying-places of our Kings and heroes, and to look up to the height where the last Abbot of that great house won the martyr's crown rather than betray his trust and provide for his own enrichment and promotion by wilfully surrendering his church to the illegal bidding of the spoiler.([40])

But we have now chiefly to see how these various changes affected the constitution and position of our church of Wells. As Wells was a secular foundation, the suppression of the monasteries did not touch it at all; Glastonbury and Bath fell, but Wells went on just as it had done before. If anything, the church of Wells gained by the suppression, as it was thereby restored to the rank which it held before the days of John de Villulâ. As I have already said, the church of Bath was suppressed along with the other monasteries, and the Chapter of Wells was once more made, by an Act of Parliament in 1543, the sole Chapter of the Somersetshire Bishoprick.([41]) It is undoubtedly true that, for three years, from 1537 to 1540, the Deanery was irregularly held by the King's favourite, Lord Cromwell, who, of course, as a layman, could not perform its duties.([42]) This was a great abuse, but it was not altogether a new abuse. To search no further, earlier in Henry's reign the two Deaneries of Exeter and Wimborne had been held at once by the King's cousin, Reginald Pole, who was afterwards Cardinal and Archbishop, but who had not then taken holy orders. Reginald Pole was, to be sure, a theological student, a description which would hardly apply to Thomas Cromwell; still Pole could as little discharge the duties of Dean of Exeter as Cromwell could discharge those of Dean of Wells.([43]) It was not till the reign of Edward the Sixth that the systematic picking and stealing from ecclesiastical bodies, as distinguished from their regular suppression, set in like a flood. The first instalment of destruction was indeed done in a regular and legal way. In his first year (1547), all chantries and colleges were suppressed, the cathedral chapters, the colleges in the Universities, and a few others only being spared.(44) The suppression of the chantries, where masses were said for the souls of particular persons, necessarily followed on the change of doctrine; but the general suppression of Colleges, which had the effect of destroying the capitular bodies at Beverley, Wimborne, and a crowd of other places, was sheer destruction, and not reformation. Then came the general plunder of Bishopricks, Chapters, and ecclesiastical bodies generally, which began under Edward, and went on again in a form one degree less shameless under Elizabeth. A Bishop was commonly bullied into exchanging the estates of his see for some pretended equivalent, commonly in the shape of impropriate tithes. No church suffered in this way more than that of Wells. William Barlow, who became Bishop in 1547, the first year of Edward the Sixth, was driven in the course of that year and the next to give up to Edward Duke of Somerset pretty well everything belonging to the see, including the palace of Wells itself, in exchange for a few rectories.(45) A large part of this property was lost for ever; but a good deal was recovered by Barlow himself after the Duke's execution, and by his successor Gilbert Bourne in the days of Queen Mary.(46) It is not easy for us to conceive that there was a time when the palace had ceased to be the house of the Bishop, and had become the dwelling of a lay nobleman. And when we remember that that lay nobleman, besides receiving endless estates elsewhere, was also the grantee and the destroyer of the Abbey of Glastonbury, we get a good specimen of the way in which the property of the Church was squandered away, not for the public good in any shape, but for the private enrichment of greedy courtiers. Of the other foundations in Wells, the Priory of Saint John had fallen in 1541. This, I should explain, though its chief officer bore the title of Prior, was not a monastery, but a hospital.(⁴⁷) The college of Chantry-priests fell by the Act of 1547; (⁴⁸) the plunderers then fell upon the property of the Chapter and of its individual members. The estates of the Deanery were swallowed up, and, in order to patch up a new endowment for the Dean, an Act was passed for the suppression of the offices of Provost and Sub-Chanter, the estates of which formed a new corps for the Deanery.(⁴⁹) But as with the lands of the Bishoprick, so with those of the Deanery, a great part was recovered in the days of Queen Mary; so that, as the provostship and sub-chantership were never restored, I suspect that the Deans in the end gained by their spoliation. Some of the common possessions of the Chapter were also lost, and were partly recovered by Bishop Bourne, as also were the lands of the Archdeaconry; but the Archdeacon's house of which I have already spoken has remained alienated to this day.(⁵⁰)

These are specimens of the spoliations, many of them positively illegal, all of them wrought, not for the public good but for private enrichment, which our Bishopricks, Chapters, and other ecclesiastical foundations underwent in the course of the sixteenth century. But at Wells these spoliations had an important effect on the constitution of the church. Legal cavils were raised as to the right both of the Chapter and the Vicars to their possessions. It was affirmed that the reconstitution of the Deanery had somehow involved the complete suppression of the Chapter. Both the Chapter and the College of Vicars therefore found it expedient to procure charters from Queen Elizabeth confirming them in their rights and properties. The charter granted to the Chapter is a most curious document, because it is evident that the Residentiaries took this opportunity to procure something like a legal confirmation of the usurpations by which the non-residentiary Canons were gradually cheated out of their rights and powers. The Queen refounds all the dignities and prebends, and endows them afresh with their old possessions. Then, as if the holders of these dignities and prebends did not form the Chapter, the Charter goes on to found the Chapter, as a body consisting of Residentiaries only, and to grant to them the cathedral church and other property. The deed winds up by saying that the non-residentiary Canons are to have votes in Chapter, but only for the purpose of electing a Bishop.([31]) I do not profess to know what may be the legal force of such a document, though it certainly seems to me that nothing short of an Act of Parliament can take away from any man or any corporation any rights which they already legally enjoy. But whatever it may be worth, this charter is the authority for the practice by which at Wells the non-residentiary Canons are summoned to the election of a Bishop and not to other meetings of the Chapter, while at

York they are still summoned to every meeting. I am not a lawyer and I do not speak as one. But historically the thing is a cheat and an usurpation. The Elizabethan charter carries its own contradiction with it; and, as an ecclesiastical reformer, I say once more that the point to be most strongly insisted on, if our cathedral bodies are ever again to fulfil their ancient uses, is to make both classes of Canons realities. The Residentiaries must be Residentiaries, living on the spot, not making the cathedral a place of holiday retirement from duties elsewhere. And lest the smaller body of Residentiaries should again sink into a narrow oligarchy, the whole body of Canons must be again restored to their ancient rights, not only in the formal election of a Bishop, but in all those matters of election, patronage, discipline, and business of every kind, which are expressed in the ancient formula of "a stall in the choir and a voice in the chapter-house." (52)

On the two following centuries I need not dwell. I will rather hasten on to our own times. The last great changes in the church of Wells come within our own memory. Those changes say a great deal for the zeal and energy of those who carried them out, but they say very little for their taste and knowledge. The pity is that they were done at the particular time when they were done, when it was quite possible to get detail well executed—and the detail certainly is very well executed—but when ecclesiastical arrangement was not understood. It would have been far better to have let the church remain in its old state, wretched as that state was, for twenty or thirty years longer. As it was, the change was made in one sense so badly as to make the whole thing a by-word, in another sense so well that I fear there is little chance of undoing it for a good while to come. Some things were done which were deeds of sheer havoc, deeds worthy of no one but of Protector Somerset himself. What had those Bishops done whose figures may be seen in the undercroft of the Chapter-house, that they should be torn away from their places and shut up as it were in a posthumous dungeon? What had our famous Beckington done that his canopy should be carried away, and set up where, as covering nothing, it is simply ridiculous and unmeaning? To be sure even that was not the lowest depth in store for the great benefactor. His canopy had yet to be mutilated and moved backwards and forwards in order the better to display the most hideous stoves with which human perversity ever disfigured an ancient building.([53]) When we think of the havoc of last year, one is half inclined to forgive the havoc of twenty years back. Yet one cannot help asking why the long continuous ranges of stalls which give such dignity to the choirs of Winchester, Ely, and Manchester, were forsaken for the absurd arrangement which sticks the stalls piecemeal between the pillars, and which so lessens their numbers that, if the whole Chapter were ever to assemble, some less lucky Canons must sit on the laps of others? ([54]) Why was all this done? I know the answer well. It was to provide room for the congregation; it was thought a great feat to give a little more width to the choir, and so to gain a few more sittings, by putting the stalls between the pillars instead of in their proper place in front of them. Now to provide for the congregation is an excellent object, but the wisdom of our forefathers had already found ample room for the congregation in quite another way. Did those who planned the last arrangements of Wells Cathedral know that there was a nave, and, if they did know it, for what end did they suppose that that nave was built? A Bishop, coming in by the cloister door, might possibly never find out that there was a nave at all; but a Dean, coming in at the west end, must have seen that there was a good deal of building between that door and his own stall, and one would have thought that he must sometimes have stopped to think for what end that building was set up. Was that long array of arches, that soaring vault, made simply as a place for rubbing shoes before the service begins or for chattering after the service is ended? I think that Robert and Jocelin had better notions of the adaptation of means to ends than to rear so great a work for such small purposes. When the last changes were made at Wells, these elementary questions seem not to have presented themselves to men's minds. Had the work waited till now, Wells might not have been, as it now is, a reproach and a proverb among the minsters of England, but we might have held our place alongside of our fellows at Chichester and Hereford and Lichfield and Llandaff. The truth, simple as it is, though it seems so strange to many minds, is that the nave of a cathedral, no less than of any other church, is nothing in the world but the place for the congregation. There is something wonderful in the kind of difficulty which some people seem to have in taking in so plain a fact. It is a thing which I have said over and over again, and people stare and seem not to know what I mean. Yet I am not putting forth any dream of my own; I am saying what is a sober fact in many other places, and what might easily be made a sober fact at Wells also. I do not ask you to go to the ends of the earth; I do not ask you even to go to places like Ely and Durham in distant parts of our island. A short trip will take you to Llandaff, and a trip a little longer will take you to Hereford, and there you will see English cathedral churches as they ought to be, but as the church of Wells is not. Enter the church of Wells, you find yourself in a vast empty space; a solid wall in front of you, with an organ on the top of it, blocks off the small part of the church which alone is used for divine worship. Into that small part, designed originally for the clergy and choir only, the whole congregation is rammed, jammed, crammed without distinction; or rather there is distinction, and too much distinction, but it is distinction wholly of the wrong kind. Can the small space in which we find ourselves be the common church of the diocese, the church of the Bishop, the church of his flock? Alas! it looks far too much like the private chapel of some half-dozen clergymen and their private friends. Think too of the burning shame of appropriated seats in a cathedral choir. The gold ring and the goodly apparel soon find their way to the chief seats of the synagogue, while the poor man in vile raiment is bidden by an unconscious irony to go and further crowd up the space which should be left void to give dignity to the approach to God's altar. Is this the way to make the whole people of the diocese feel at home in the temple which was built for them? Is this the way to strengthen a Church which seems to shrink from proclaiming itself as the Church of the People, and which seems to clutch at the shadowy dignity of being the Church of the exclusive few? Ten arches of nave stand empty, and the worshipper seeking a place has to ask, "Is this or the other person likely to come to-day?" before the spot sacred to exclusiveness may be safely intruded on. Cross the Channel, and you will see another sight. Enter by the western door of the church of Llandaff, and right before your eyes stands the altar, raised aloft in fitting majesty. Below it, open to all eyes, is the Bishop on his throne, the clergy and singers in their stalls. The long nave is filled with the people, the faithful of the city and diocese. Nothing distinguishes worshippers of higher worldly position; nothing distinguishes the households of the dignitaries of the cathedral from their fellow Christians of lower degree. There is the church as it should be; ([55]) can we apply that name to our own church as it is? Here is the great reform; here is the one great work to be done. Make the church once more a church, before we trouble ourselves with the enrichments of the building. Make clean the inside of the cup and the platter, and the adornment of the outside may come afterwards.([56]) Do not misunderstand me; do not think I am asking for the wretched half-and-half mockery which is called "service in the nave." We know what that means; we see it once or twice in the year; it means a return to chaos. It means a sham altar, sham stalls, sham everything. At the very times when an unusual number of the cathedral clergy are present, it is impossible for them to take their proper places, and they are driven higgledy-piggledy into the places of the congregation. What I want is service in the nave and in the choir at once. Then comes the answer, "Oh, but it is impossible; the screen is in the way." The remedy is easy; pull the screen down.([57]) There are churches where so simple a remedy could not be so easily applied. In churches of the vast size of Canterbury, York, and Winchester, where also the screen is often a work of great antiquity and architectural beauty, there are no doubt real difficulties in the way of carrying out the scheme for which I am fighting. The close screen, shutting off the choir from the nave, was in its right place in a monastery, where the church really belonged to the monks, where the people were present only by sufferance, and where the monks needed some such shelter during their midnight worship. But in a cathedral church, which exists for the sake of the whole diocese, such screens were an abuse from the beginning, which ought never to have been brought in. Still we should think twice before we pulled down the ancient and splendid screens which divide the naves and choirs of some of our greater minsters. But at Wells there is no difficulty at all. The size of the church is moderate, and the screen is of no architectural value. Cut it down; why cumbereth it the ground? Break down the middle wall of partition that is against us, and let the people of the diocese of Wells again have their own church for their own. Did you not feel the lack at the last great ceremony held in this place, when our new Bishop came to take possession of his seat and to show himself as a father among his children? That ceremony, which in its very nature ought to have been done in the sight of the whole people of the diocese, could be done only in the sight of a favoured few. It was a very different sight which I saw two years back in the cathedral church of Bayeux. There I saw the installation of a new Bishop of that see,—a Bishop, I may add, who is at this moment bravely defending Gallican liberties against Roman usurpations. The rite was done in the face of the world, and the whole of that noble minster was thronged with clergy and laity from the west door to the high altar. Tell me not of impossibilities; what has been done at Lichfield and Hereford and Llandaff may be done at Wells also. I remember Llandaff a ruin; go and see for yourselves what it now is. I remember the choir of Lichfield in a far worse case than ever the choir of Wells was. I remember it blocked off from the nave, glazed and plastered, and room for the congregation found by throwing the Lady chapel into it. Go and see what the model church of England is now. "Oh, but, if we are in the nave, and if the altar is raised as it is at Llandaff, we shall not be able to see into the Lady chapel." Certainly you will not; but, of all the possible lawful and unlawful uses of a Lady chapel, that of acting as a peep-show to the choir certainly never came into the heads of its founders. But if you are not able to see the Lady chapel, you will be able to see something much better: you will be able to see what you never have seen; you will see the inside of the cathedral church itself. You will see the mighty whole, from west door to high altar, each part performing its proper function, and, as a mere view, affording a far nobler sight than the pretty peep into the eastern chapels which would be lost. And then comes another objection. "Oh, but if we are in the nave, we shall never be able to hear." *Solvitur audiendo.* If the officiating minister spouts or mumbles, of course you will not hear; if he chants as there is at least one among us who can chant, you might hear to the end of Saint Alban's Abbey. The light open screen, such as you see at Lichfield and Hereford, in no way hinders sight and hearing; and for those parts of the service for which chanting is unfit, for the sermon and the lessons, the preacher or reader would of course come out into the nave. The pulpit is ready for him, the lectern is ready for him, and the new device of a pulpit stuck so grotesquely opposite the Bishop's throne might, I should think, be swept away without anybody weeping for it. But from the elder pulpit, the quaint design of the seventeenth century, I will draw a lesson. It bears the legend, "Be instant in season, out of season," and instant in season, out of season, I will be, and let every one who thinks with me be also, till we have broken down the dull mass of prejudice and ignorance which stands in our way. We must work till we have given new life to what is not dead but only sleeping—till we have reformed our ancient institutions on their ancient principles—till we have swept away all traces of the days of greediness and ignorance—till pluralist Deans and non-resident Residentiaries have become things of the past—till the mother-church of the diocese has again become the church of the Bishop and the church of his flock, open to all, free to all, whose doors are never shut against any, and where every inch from western door to rood-screen stands ready for men not only to admire but to worship. Thus let us reform, lest others destroy. The true conservative is ever the true reformer, and the true reformer is ever the true conservative. If we would preserve the essence of our institutions, we must sweep away their abuses. And none of our institutions are nobler in their theory, none have more sadly fallen away in their practice, than our ancient cathedral churches. The Church of England is at this moment on her trial, and, above all her institutions, her cathedral foundations are pre-eminently on their trial. There never was a moment when a little more sleep and a little more slumber was less fitted to be the order of the day. Those who, with me, love and venerate those ancient fabrics and foundations, those who, by seeking their reformation, are thereby seeking their preservation, are bound to be up and doing. The work has begun; wherever there is a will, there is a way; many an ancient minster has put on a new garb, alike in its material fabric and in the worship carried on within it. Why should we lag behind our neighbours? Why should the mistakes of twenty years past be hung like a clog around our necks? Some needful reforms indeed could not be done without the legislative help, but it needs no Act of Parliament to make the nave of Wells Cathedral as truly a living thing, as truly a place of real and living worship, as the naves of Llandaff and Lichfield. A zeal not according to knowledge condemned us to the mischiefs of a restoration which was done too soon. Whenever zeal accompanied by knowledge appears in authority among us, as it has already appeared among others, the work will be done.

NOTES.

LECTURE I.

(1) "Domus eleemosynaria nobilis paupertatis" is the style of the Hospital of Saint Cross near Winchester, as enlarged by Cardinal Beaufort. See the Licence of Incorporation in the Monasticon, vii. 724.

(2) I refer to the debate in the House of Commons on the Scotch Reform Bill of 1868, when it was discussed whether Wells or Evesham should be disfranchised.

"Sir Lawrence Palk argued on behalf of Wells that it is 'a cathedral city of great antiquity.' This appeal on behalf of the seculars was at once met by the monastic zeal of Sir John Pakington, who daringly answered, that if Evesham 'cannot boast of a cathedral, it can of one of the most beautiful abbeys in England.' We should be sorry to suspect the good town of Evesham of any Anabaptist tendencies, but it is certain that, if it makes the boast which the member for Droitwich puts into its mouth, it belongs to the class of those who do falsely boast. . . . Mr. Gladstone had never been at Evesham; we know of no particular call of duty likely to take him there; but Sir John Pakington, a Worcestershire man, must surely have visited a borough in his own shire. How then about the beautiful abbey, one of the most beautiful in England? Any one who has been both at Wells and at Evesham must know that Wells Cathedral is still standing, while Evesham Abbey, saving its bell-tower and a small piece of wall, has long ceased to exist. But one might ask both disputants whether Sir Lawrence Palk, in his zeal for cathedrals, would enfranchise Ely and Saint David's—whether Sir John Pakington, in his zeal for abbeys, would restore Saint Alban's and enfranchise Romsey."—*Saturday Review*, July 11, 1868.

(3) This Lecture was given in the time between the election and installation of the present Bishop, Lord Arthur Hervey.

(4) In strictness the West-Saxon Bishoprick was first placed at Dorchester in Oxfordshire in 635, and the see was not finally settled at

Winchester till 670. The time between these years was one of great confusion. See Bæda, Hist. Eccl. iii. 7. Florence of Worcester, i. 235. Stubbs, Registrum Sacrum Anglicanum, 161.

(5) See Bæda, v. 18, and the Chronicle A.D. 709. The first Bishop at Sherborne was Ealdhelm. See his life by William of Malmesbury in Wharton, Anglia Sacra, ii. 20.

(6) See Florence of Worcester, i. 236. Will. Malm. Gesta Regum, ii. 129. Gesta Pont. in Scriptores post Bædam, 144 *b*; Canonicus Wellensis in Anglia Sacra, i. 554; Stubbs, 13.

(7) In 710 Ine won a victory over the Cornish King Gerent; in 722 Taunton is spoken of as the town which Ine had built. This fixes the foundation of Taunton within that time. See the Chronicles under these years.

(8) On this whole matter, see Anglia Sacra, i. 553, and the Historiola de Primordiis Episcopatûs Somersetensis in Hunter's Ecclesiastical Documents, p. 10. The alleged charter of Cynewulf will be found in Kemble's Codex Diplomaticus, i. 141.

(9) Ceawlin conquered to the Axe in 577; Cenwealh to the Parret in 658; Ine, as we see, as far as Taunton. On Ceawlin see Dr. Guest in the Archæological Journal, xix. 193.

(10) That is, the modern shires of Monmouth and Glamorgan.

(11) This is shown in various passages of the Laws of Ine. See Thorpe's Laws and Institutes, i. 119, 131, 147, 149.

(12) See the whole history of the early church of Glastonbury in the first chapter of Professor Willis' Architectural History of Glastonbury Abbey.

(13) See Willis' Architectural History of Canterbury, p. 20; ditto Winchester, p. 34.

(14) It is not said in so many words that the church of Dunstan was of stone, but it is plain that it was so, both because the "lignea basilica" or wooden church is distinguished from it, and because Osbern the biographer of Dunstan (Anglia Sacra, ii. 100) speaks of him as laying the foundations, which could hardly be said of a wooden church.

(15) See the account of the Canons of Waltham in the book De Inventione, and those of Rheims in Richer, iii. 24.

(16) I have discussed this in full in my History of the Norman Conquest, ii. 571, Ed. 2.

(17) When a Bishop is to be elected by the Chapter, two quite distinct documents are sent; there is first the *congé d'élire*, which recognizes the undoubted right of the Chapter to elect and gives them full leave to elect, only with a little good advice as to the sort of person to be chosen. With this, as a kind of after-thought, comes the *letter missive* or *letter recommendatory*, recommending a particular person for election.

(18) The names of the early Bishops, of whom but little is recorded, will be found in the Canon of Wells, Anglia Sacra, i. 556, and Godwin's Catalogue of English Bishops, 290.

(19) He was "natione Saxo," says his successor Gisa in the Historiola de Primordiis Episcopatûs Somersetensis. See Norman Conquest, ii. 583.

(20) See Godwin, p. 291.

(21) Anglia Sacra, i. 559.

(22) See Historiola, 15—18; Mr. J. R. Green in the Transactions of the Somersetshire Archæological and Natural History Society, 1863-4, p. 148; and Norman Conquest, ii. 674.

(23) For examples see Norman Conquest, ii. 549.

(24) See the writ, the only writ of Harold's which is preserved, in Kemble's Codex Diplomaticus, iv. 305.

(25) After mentioning Harold's promise, Gisa (Historiola, p. 18) adds, "præoccupante autem illum judicio divinæ ultionis," and goes on to speak of Harold's two battles and his death.

(26) Historiola, p. 19, "publice vivere et inhoneste mendicare necessariorum inopia antea coegerat."

(27) For the story of Hermann, see Norman Conquest, ii. 401.

(28) On these places see Historiola, pp. 18, 19. But it is as well to say that the well-known charter of Eadward to Gisa, printed in Cod. Dipl. iv. 162, is undoubtedly spurious, though it is useful as giving the names of places in the neighbourhood, in older, though not always their oldest, forms.

(29) The rule of Chrodegang will be found at length in D'Achery's Spicilegium, i. 565; and see Norman Conquest, ii. 84.

(30) This was about 969. Adalbero's changes are described at length by Richer, iii. 24, in Pertz's smaller collection.

(31) See Norman Conquest, ii. 84.

(32) In Domesday Book, pp. 89—89 *b*, the land of the canons is put under that of the Bishop; "Canonici Sancti Andreæ tenent de Episcopo." This is much the same with the Canons of Exeter in p. 101 *b*. In the Exon Domesday, (71) "Isaac præpositus Canonicorum Sancti Andreæ" is mentioned by name.

(33) Historiola, 21: "Sepultus est in ecclesiâ quam rexerat, in hemicyclo [a semicircle or round arch] facto in pariete a parte aquilonali prope altare, sicut Duduco prædecessor ejus sepultus est a meridie juxta altare."

(34) Will. Malms. Gest. Regg. iii. 300. "Pronunciatum est secundum dicta canonum ut episcopi transeuntes de villis constituerent sedes suas in urbibus diœcesium suarum." This was in 1072, but the change at Wells did not take place just yet.

In his other book, the Gesta Pontificum (144 *b*), he says that John "minoris gloriæ putans si in villâ resideret inglorius, transferre thronum in Bathoniam animo intendit."

(35) William of Malmesbury, in the place last quoted, says, "Cessit enim Andreas Simoni fratri, frater major minori."

(36) See the Chronicles under 577, and note 9.

(37) The charters are given in Dugdale's Monasticon, ii. 66, 67. In the second charter of Henry the First he speaks of "Batha ubi frater meus Willielmus et ego constituimus et confirmavimus sedem episcopatûs totius Summersetæ, quæ olim erat apud villam quæ dicitur Wella." The grant of the town which is confirmed in this charter of Henry is made in a charter of William Rufus on the same page.

(38) So says William of Malmesbury in the passage last quoted: "Aliquantum dure in monachos agebat, quod essent hebetes et ejus æstimatione barbari."

(39) The Historiola mentions the destruction of Gisa's buildings, and the Canon of Wells adds (Anglia Sacra, i. 560), "Fundum in quo prius habitabant sibi et suis successoribus usurpavit, palatiumque suum episcopale ibidem construxit."

(40) See Willis' Architectural History of Winchester, 34, 35.

(41) Historiola, p. 22. "Canonici foras ejecti coacti sunt cum populo communiter vivere."

(42) The story of Hildebert, John, and the Provostship is given both in the Historiola and by the Canon of Wells. Several letters discussing the matter appeared in the Gentleman's Magazine in the year 1864 in

the numbers for February, July, August, September, October, November, and December, especially one by Mr. Stubbs in November.

That Hildebert was the brother of Bishop John appears from a charter of Bishop Robert (which I shall have to quote again) in the Monasticon, ii. 293, where Bishop John is called the uncle of Precentor Reginald.

(43) This comes afterwards in the Historiola, p. 24.

(44) The Canon (p. 560) says, "Licet ipse confractus senio inde pœniteret, tamen ædificia canonicorum destructa minime reparavit, nec fundum eis injuste ablatum restituit." But the Historiola seems to imply at least a purpose of restitution, as its words are, "Pœnitentiâ ductus de sacrilegio perpetrato, resipuit et pœnituit, et pœnitentiam suam scriptam reliquit. Johannes vero Archidiaconus terras quas pater suus obtinuerat per hæreditatem et præposituram canonicorum nihilominus sibi usurpavit."

(45) The Charter is printed in the Monasticon, ii. 268.

LECTURE II.

(1) The Historiola and the Canon both call Godfrey simply "Teutonicus;" but it appears from the Continuator of Florence of Worcester (ii. 78) and from the Annals of Waverley (Ann. Mon. ii. 219) that he was Chancellor to Queen Adeliza. We can hardly doubt that he was one of her countrymen from the Netherlands.

(2) This account of him is given both by the Historiola and by the Canon (Angl. Sacr. i. 561), who gives as a reason for his mission to Glastonbury, "eo quod non recte eorum aratra incedebant." His birth comes from the Continuator of Florence (ii. 95), who says that he was "Flandrensis genere, sed natus in partibus Angliæ."

(3) Historiola, p. 25.

(4) See the agreement in Wharton's note, Anglia Sacra, i. 561.

(5) The Act is printed in the Monasticon, ii. 293.

(6) Historiola, p. 24: "Ipse ecclesiam Beati Petri Apostoli de Bathoniâ magnis cū expensis construi fecit."

(7) Angl. Sacr. i. 561: "Complevit fabricam ecclesiæ Bathoniensis per Johannem Turonensem inchoatam." This seems to be confirmed by the words of John himself in the charter which I have already quoted (Monasticon, ii. 268), which is dated in 1116, and where he says

that he sets aside the revenues of the city of Bath "ad perficiendum novum opus quod incepi."

(8) Historiola, p. 24: "Capitulum quoque et claustrum, dormitorium et refectorium et infirmatorium, nihilominus ædificari fecit."

(9) Historiola, p. 24. See above, p. 39.

(10) The Historiola (p. 25) mentions only the Deanery and Precentorship as founded by Robert. "Decanatum in ecclesiâ constituit, et Decanum et Præcentorem primos ordinavit." But the Canon (p. 561) says, "Ordinavit etiam in ecclesiâ Wellensi Decanum et Subdecanum, Præcentorem et Succentorem, Thesaurarium et Cancellarium, *quem vocavit Archiscolam* in statutis ecclesiæ Wellensis, quæ ipse primus edidit omnium in eâdem." (Robert, the first to make the Chapter a distinct corporation, was naturally its first lawgiver.) He adds, "Tum Decanus, Subdecanus, etc. non habebant tunc temporis illa beneficia eis annexa, quæ eorum successores nunc habent in ecclesiâ antedictâ." But in the deed by which Bishop Robert founds the Deanery and divides the estates of the church into prebends (Monasticon, ii. 293), no dignitary is mentioned except the Dean and Precentor; and the church of Wookey, which afterwards belonged to the Sub-Dean, is specially mentioned as belonging to the Dean. This certainly looks as if Robert had founded the Deanery and Precentorship only. But, if they were not founded by Robert, they were founded by Jocelin, for the Canon says (564), "Jocelinus fundavit multas præbendas in ecclesiâ Wellensi de novo, dotavit etiam omnes dignitates, personatus, et officia dictæ ecclesiæ, in formâ adhuc durante."

The duties of the different officers of the church cannot be better described than they are by Bishop Godwin (p. 294): "He also it was that first constituted a Deane to be the President of the Chapter, and a Subdeane to supply his place in absence; a Chaunter to governe the quier, and a Subchaunter under him; a *Chauncellour to instruct the yoonger sort of Cannons:* and lastly a Treasurer to looke to the ornaments of the church." He adds, "The Subchauntership togither with the Provostship an. 1547. were taken away and suppressed by Act of Parliament, to patch up a Deanry, the lands and revenewes of the Deanry being devoured by sacrilegious cormorants."

(11) He did what he did "consilio et auxilio illustris Regis Stephani et venerabilis Episcopi Henrici," says the Historiola, p. 24.

(12) That is, in the churches of Bangor and Saint Asaph, and now in those of Saint David's and Llandaff. But, till the late changes, there were no Deans at Saint David's and Llandaff, beyond a vague tradition

that the Bishop was Dean. At Saint David's the Precentor was President of the Chapter and at Llandaff the Archdeacon. The collegiate church of Southwell had no Dean or President under any title.

(13) A *sinecure* is strictly an office *sine curâ animarum*, without cure of souls, not necessarily an office where there is nothing to do of any kind.

(14) See the quotation in note 10.

(15) I here alluded to the Theological College, where the offices of Principal and Vice-Principal are held by the Sub-Dean of the cathedral and another Canon, who are therefore really resident, but who are not admitted to any share in those rights and revenues which go to those nominal Residentiaries who stay away nine months in the year.

(16) *Beneficium* is the word constantly used for a lay fief as well as for an ecclesiastical living. The most curious instance of this use will be found in the dispute between Pope Hadrian the Fourth and the Emperor Frederick Barbarossa. The Pope speaks of his coronation of the Emperor as a "beneficium" conferred on him. The German Bishops were very indignant, as if the Pope meant that the Empire was a fief of the Papacy. The Pope then explains that "beneficium" means both *benefit* and *benefice*. He thought that he had done the Emperor a *benefit* by crowning him, but he did not pretend to invest him with a *benefice*. See the History of Frederick by Otto (continued by Radevic) of Freisingen, ii. 15, 16, 22. Most likely the Pope used an ambiguous word on purpose.

(17) Compare the account in the Historiola, p. 24, with Robert's charter quoted above.

(18) See the Historiola, pp. 26, 27. The story begins in a marked way. "Quum . . . deinceps, glorioso Rege Stephano decedente, Rex præpotens Henricus secundus regni gubernacula suscepisset."

(19) Domesday Book and the Codex Diplomaticus are full of such cases.

(20) His words (Monasticon, ii. 293) are: "Quum igitur ecclesiam Wellensem indebitis præpositura oppressionibus supra modum afflictam invenimus et gravatam, communicato consilio archiepiscoporum, episcoporum, aliarumque religiosarum Angliæ personarum, exigentibus quoque ejusdem ecclesiæ canonicis, Decanum illic ordinavimus, concessis sibi dignitatibus, libertatibus, et consuetudinibus canonicis ecclesiarum Angliæ bene ordinatarum, et ne in eâdem ecclesiâ pristina tribulatio locum denuo vendicaret, possessiones et prædia quæ ad eam fidelium sunt donatione devoluta in præbendas taliter distribuimus."

"Rogerus Witene," who must, one would think, have been one of the same stock, appears in the Exeter Domesday, p. 75, as a tenant of the Church of Glastonbury.

(21) See the letter of Bishop Rowland Lee to Lord Cromwell in the Monasticon, iii. 199. He prays that it might be "browghte to a college churche as Liche [Lichfield]."

(22) On this point, and on other points touching the relations of Bishops and Chapters, there was much disputing between Robert Grosseteste, the great Bishop of Lincoln, contemporary with our Jocelin, and his Canons. See on the Chapter's side, Matthew Paris, pp. 485, 522, 572 ; and, on the other, Robert's own letter to his Chapter in Mr. Luard's collection of his Letters, p. 357.

(23) The words of the Historiola, p. 24, are, "Porro non est oblivioni tradendum quod ecclesia Welliæ suo consilio fabricata est et auxilio." The Canon (561) says only, "Multas ruinas ejusdem ecclesiæ destructiones ejus in locis pluribus comminantes egregie reparavit."

(24) "Ecclesiam sedis meæ perspiciens esse mediocrem," he says in the Historiola, p. 16.

(25) The consecration and the presence of the three Bishops is mentioned both in the Historiola and by the Canon.

(26) William of Malmesbury, writing not very long before Robert's time, says of the church of Eadward at Westminster (ii. 228), "Quam ipse illo compositionis genere primus in Angliâ ædificaverat quod nunc pene cuncti sumptuosis æmulantur expensis." Matthew Paris (2), evidently copying this, alters the tense, because in his day another style of architecture had come in. His words are, "Quam ipse novo compositionis genere construxerat, a quâ post multi ecclesias construentes, exemplum adepti, opus illud expensis *æmulabantur* sumptuosis."

(27) The Canon of Wells (Angl. Sacr. i. 562) says of him, "Multas præbendas in ecclesiâ Wellensi fundavit de novo, multaque alia bona fecit tam Bathoniensi quam Wellensi ecclesiis." He mentions also his gift of the manor of North Curry and other lands to the Chapter, and speaks of him as granting the first municipal rights to the citizens of Wells, a point which I must leave to Mr. Serel.

(28) See Mr. Stubbs' account of Savaric in the Gentleman's Magazine for November 1863, p. 621, and Mr. Green's notice in the Transactions of the Somersetshire Archæological and Natural History Society for 1863, p. 39.

(29) The whole history is given at length by Adam of Domersham, a monk of Glastonbury, in Anglia Sacra, i. 578.

(30) See Anglia Sacra, i. 579. The Dean was Alexander, the third Dean.

(31) See the disputes about the "advocatio" or "patronatus" of the Abbey in Anglia Sacra, i. 584, and the correspondence between Bishop Beckington and Abbot Frome, translated by Mr. George Williams in the Somersetshire Proceedings, 1863, p. 17. On the terms of the composition see pp. 564, 585.

(32) See Roger of Wendover, iii. 222.

(33) Anglia Sacra, i. 564. "Capellas etiam cum cameris de Welles et Woky notabiliter construxit." In the Palace at Wells, Jocelin's chapel has been reconstructed, and many buildings added by later Bishops, but the greater part of the house is still his. In Wookey Court, now a farmhouse and alienated from the see, only a single doorway, probably that of the chapel, remains of Jocelin's work, but it is in exactly the same style as the Palace and the West Front of the Cathedral.

(34) See Matthew Paris, p. 756, ed. Wats. He describes the earthquake as happening four days before Christmas, and says that he had the account of what happened at Wells from the Bishop himself. This must be William Button the First, who however could not have been at Wells at the time, as he was consecrated at Rome on June 14 in that year and did not come back to England till the next year. His account of the damage at Wells stands thus, "Tholus quoque lapideus magnæ quantitatis et ponderis, qui per diligentiam cæmentariorum in summitate ecclesiæ de Welles ponebatur, raptus de loco suo, non sine damno, super ecclesiam cecidit, et quum ab alto ruerit, tumultum reddens horribilem audientibus timorem incussit non minimum. In quo etiam terræ motu hoc accidit mirabile; caminorum, propugnaculorum, et columnarum capitella et summitates motæ sunt, bases vero et fundamenta nequaquam, quum contrarium naturaliter debuit evenire." Yet in the repairs of the nave of Wells, a greater change seems to have been made in the bases of the pillars than in their capitals.

(35) Matthew Paris gives the list, p. 522, Abingdon, Wells, Evesham, Gloucester, Tewkesbury, Winchcomb (?), Pershore, Alcester, "et multæ aliæ per regnum Angliæ."

(36) These were various works in the church and dormitory, done in the time of Abbot William, 1214-1235. Matthew Paris, in the Gesta Abbatum (i. 280), after describing them, adds, "Quippe ista conquæstu

et industriâ Ricardi de Thidenhangaer, monachi nostri conversi ac camerarii, sine obedientiæ suæ defectu vel diminutione, sunt perfecta: *quæ tamen Abbati ob reverentiam sunt adscribenda.* Ille enim facit, cujus auctoritate quippiam fieri dinoscitur."

(37) In the Historia Monasterii S. Petri Gloucestriæ (i. 29) we read, " Et anno Domini MCCXLII. completa est nova volta in navi ecclesiæ, non auxilio fabrorum ut primo, sed animosâ virtute monachorum item in ipso loco exsistentiam."

(38) See especially Gervase's account of the architects employed at Canterbury, William of Sens and William the Englishman ; Willis, 35, 51.

(39) Mr. Serel gives me a reference to the Close Rolls of Henry the Third, October 3, 1225, in which "the King grants to the Bishop of Bath five marks towards the works in the church of Wells, the same payment to be continued for the eleven following years according to the King's gift."

(40) The extract is given in the Monasticon, ii. 278. It consists of a series of regulations touching the keeping open and shut of various doors. The door of which I speak is described as " magnum ostium ecclesiæ *sub campanili* versus claustrum." This must mean the door in the transept, under the great central tower, rather than the door opening into the cloister from the south-western tower. But the existence of the cloister is proved by the mention of either, and it is equally odd to call either of them " magnum ostium ecclesiæ."

Another doorway in the cloister is also spoken of in the same document ; "Ostium *versus capellam Beatæ Virginis in claustro* propter cameram necessariam." This door, I imagine, may still be traced in the east walk of the cloister, near the remains of the Lady chapel in the cloister. This chapel must be carefully distinguished from the Lady chapel at the east end of the church. Mention is also made of "duo ostia *de la Karole,* ex utráque parte chori," one of which is further described as "ostium *de la Karole versus librariam.*" The word *Karole* or *Carel* has several meanings ; but it generally implies a small recess or chamber of some kind. Were the books kept in one of the transepts?

Another mention of the Lady chapel in the cloister is found in Anglia Sacra, i. 566, when Bishop William Button the First, who died in 1264, is said to have buried " in novâ capellâ B. Mariæ Virginis." On this Professor Willis (Somersetshire Proceedings, 1863, p. 21) remarks : " As his chantry was in the 'Capella B. Virginis infra claustrum' (Liber B, p. 62), the above passage does not apply to any Lady chapel at the east of the cathedral, but to the building of the other Lady chapel, which was in the east walk of the cloister in the position usually given to a chapter-house." By "usually" the Professor must mean in monastic foundations. "Liber B" is one of the books in possession of the Chapter.

(41) See the extract in note 10.

(42) The whole passage (pp. 65, 66) is most remarkable. The writer is inveighing against Hugh, Bishop of Chester (or Lichfield), who had removed the monks from the church of Coventry, and put in secular canons. "Ædificaverant certatim etiam absentes canonici circa ecclesiam ampla et excelsa diversoria, ad usus forte proprios, si vel semel in vitâ locum visitandi caussam casus offerret. Nullus ibi ex præbendariis, sicut nec alibi faciunt, religiose resedit, sed pauperibus vicariis ad insultandum Deo modicâ mercede conductis, pro foribus palatiorum facientes magnalia, sanctum eis chorum victosque Penates et nudos ecclesiæ parietes crediderunt. Hæc est vere vera religio, hanc omnis imitari et æmulari deberet ecclesia. Canonico sæculari ab ecclesiâ suâ, quamdiu libuerit, licebit abesse, et patrimonium Christi ubi, et quando, et in quascumque voluerit voluptates absumere. Id tantum provideant, ut audiatur vociferatio frequens in domo Domini. Si ad fores talium pulsaverit advena, si pauper clamaverit, respondebit qui pro foribus habitat, (et ipse satis pauper vicarius,) 'Transite, et alibi alimoniam quærite, quia dominus domûs domi non est.' Hæc est illa gloriosa clericorum religio, cujus gratiâ Cestrensis episcopus monachos suos de Coventreiâ expulit, primus hominum tantum nefas ausus admittere. Caussâ clericorum irregulariter regularium, scilicet canonicorum, ad placitum monachos eliminavit; monachos, qui non vicario, sed ore proprio laudabant Dominum, qui habitabant et ambulabant in domo Domini cum consensu omnibus diebus vitæ suæ, qui præter victum et vestitum nihil terrenum noverant, quorum panis semper præsto fuit pauperi, quorum porta cuilibet viatori quolibet tempore patuit : nec tamen taliter placuerunt episcopo, qui numquam dilexit monachos vel monachatum."

(43) The account is given by William Fitz-Stephen, Giles, i. 257. The officiating priest is described as "quidam vicarius, Vitalis nomine, homo timoratus et honestus sacerdos." Berengar, the Archbishop's emissary, addresses him, "Non est hic hujus sedis Episcopus, sed neque Decanus : video te hic ministrum Jesu Christi."

(44) Angl. Sac. i. 564 : "Vicarios in ecclesiâ singulis Præbendariis ordinavit, tribus exceptis quibus non provisit morte præventus."

Mr. Haddan, in the new collection of Councils and Ecclesiastical Documents (i. 393), prints an account of the Church of Llandaff, 1193—1218. Bishop Henry of Abergavenny founded fourteen prebends, the duties of eight of which were to be discharged ("defungi debent") by Priest Vicars ("Vicarii Sacerdotes"), four by Deacons, and two by Subdeacons. The fourteen Vicars have now dwindled to two.

(45) Ang. Sacr. i. 563. "Hic erexit ecclesias parochiales de Ilmestre et Longe-Sutton in præbendas ecclesiæ Wellensis; quarum primam Abbati de Muchelney, secundam Abbati de Athelney et eorum successoribus contulit in perpetuam possidendas." These prebends no longer exist, having vanished along with the monasteries by whose Abbots they were held.

(46) This most important statute is printed in the Monasticon, ii. pp. 291, 292. Its date is 1242, the thirty-seventh year of Jocelin's episcopate. He records what he had done for the fabric of the church, which he found dangerous by reason of age ("periculum ruinæ patiebatur pro suâ vetustate." See above, p. 67). He had built, enlarged, and consecrated it ("ædificare cœpimus et ampliare, in quâ . . adeo profecimus, quod ipsam . . . consecravimus"). Then he goes on to say that the common ("communa") revenues of the ministers of the church had hitherto been scanty ("tenuis et insufficiens"), and that he had done much to enlarge it. It would seem then that the greater part of the estates of the church had been cut up into separate prebends, and that, before Jocelin's gift, the Chapter as a body kept but little. He then recites the consent of the Dean and Chapter to his ordinance in words which mark a very different relation between the Bishop and his Chapter from what had been in the days of Gisa and John of Tours. The change is made "consensu Johannis Sarraceni, Decani, et Capituli nostri Wellensis, qui pure et simpliciter et absolute, de merâ et spontaneâ voluntate suâ, nostræ super hoc se supposuerunt ordinationi et statuto." Then come the rules by which the Bishop, the Dean and the other dignitaries, the other Canons, and the Vicars, were on each day of residence to receive certain sums of money. They had hitherto received their daily portion, partly in money, partly in bread. The amount was now raised, and it was paid wholly in money. The Bishop had thirteen pence, the Dean and other dignitaries twelve pence, each simple Canon sixpence, each Vicar a penny, for each day of residence. At the end of the year the overplus was to be divided among those Canons who had kept the prescribed residence, which is thus defined: "Residentes autem interpretamur quoad participationem residui in fine anni omnes illos Canonicos qui *per medium annum*, sive continue sive interpolatim,

fecerint in villam [sic] residentiam, præter Decanum, Præcentorem, Cancellarium, et Thesaurarium, quos interpretamur residentes si *per duas partes anni* fecerint residentiam sive continue sive interpolatim."

Each Canon had thus three available sources of income, his own prebend, the daily distribution, and the distribution at the end of the year. The first was irrespective of residence, the latter two depended on residence.

(47) I have to thank Mr. Serel for a manuscript extract containing some details of this strange practice, as it stood at Wells. In the fourteenth century the custom was that each Canon, at the beginning of his residence, should feast the Bishop, Dean, Canons, Vicars, and all other officers of the church ("quoscumque alios dictæ ecclesiæ ministros"), at a cost which often reached two hundred marks (133*l*. 6*s*. 8*d*.), or even a hundred and fifty pounds; sums which, at the then value of money, must have been enormous, and which contrast strikingly with the pence and loaves of the older daily distribution. In a bull of Pope Boniface the Ninth, in the year 1400, this custom is condemned; it is pronounced to be "consuetudo quæ corruptela potius est dicenda," and he speaks of the cost as "inutiles sumptus ac expensæ." Instead of this waste upon eating and drinking, each simple Canon, on his admission to residence, is to pay a hundred marks, and each dignitary a hundred and fifty, to the maintenance of the fabric, and the support of the other burthens of the church ("in subsidium sustentationis fabricæ et relevamen supportationis aliorum onerum"). This was a very heavy tax, and might hinder many from residing; still, at least, the money went to a good end. This was presently so interpreted that the Dean and Residentiaries gave out of each sum so paid ten marks to the fabric, ten to the Vicars, and divided the rest among themselves. This practice was confirmed by a second bull of Pope Nicolas the Fifth, in 1433; and these regulations were confirmed by Henry the Eighth in 1539, at the advice of Lord Cromwell, who, it is not to be forgotten, would, as Dean (see p. 148), receive a share of the spoil.

Notwithstanding the commutation of the burthen from a feast to a fixed sum of money, it appears that it again became usual, "not only to pay these sums of money upon admission to a Canonry [that is, on admission to residence], but also to make a prodigious entertainment for the Bishop, Dean and Chapter [meaning the Dean and Residentiaries], the Prebendaries in town, Vicars, Proctors of the Court, and Officers of the church, *and their wives*, and also for the Mayor and Corporation, and other principal inhabitants of the Liberty and City."

The Canons' and Vicars' wives were certainly not contemplated either by Pope Boniface or by King Harry.

(48) This and all other points in the constitution of the Chapter of Saint David's has been treated of by Archdeacon Jones, in our History of Saint David's, p. 310, et seqq. The Saint David's history is throughout worth comparing with the Wells' history.

(49) In the Charter of Elizabeth, of which I shall have to speak again, each of eight Residentiaries is required to reside three months in the year; and, if a Dignitary, four. This arrangement would always give two Canons at least in residence at once.

(50) The round, rather than polygonal, chapter-house at Worcester, where the style is still Romanesque, is probably the earliest example, and that at Howden the latest. Lincoln, Westminster, Salisbury, Lichfield, and Margam, are also examples. The earlier and later chapter-houses, as at Canterbury, Durham, Bristol, and Exeter, are oblong, sometimes with an apsidal end.

(51) The grandest example of these undercrofts that I know of is under the dormitory of Battle Abbey. The arrangements of the church were ruled by the position of the high altar, which marked the site of the English standard. The result was that the dormitory was driven over the side of the hill, and had therefore to be supported by an undercroft, which at the extreme southern end rises to a prodigious height.

The undercroft of the Wells chapter-house is no more a crypt than the undercroft of the palace, or than the chapter-house at Llandaff, which simply consists of four bays of vaulting, with a central pillar, just like many undercrofts of this kind.

The undercroft of the palace at Wells has its parallel at an earlier time in the magnificent example of Romanesque date in the Bishop's palace at Angers.

(52) I must here quote Professor Willis, as reported in the Bristol Volume, p. xxviii. "The first thing to be noticed is under date 1286, when a Chapter was called together, and there was laid before them the urgent necessity which appeared from the state of the church, not only that the new structure, which had been a long time begun, should be finished, but that the whole fabric might be repaired and sustained, and such new constructions as were requisite be carried out. In 1286, however, comparing the probable date of the building which I suppose to be called the new structure, it can only be the chapter-house; and the lower part of it, commonly called the crypt, was, as I conclude, then completed. . . . . . The structure of the chapter-house consists of two parts, and it is quite evident that the crypt was separated from the upper part by a very considerable interval. I conceive, therefore, that in 1286 the portion of the chapter-house called the crypt was completed."

In the Somersetshire Transactions, xii. 19, the Professor adds that "it was agreed that each Canon should pay a tenth of his prebend yearly for five years."

Bishop Godwin says (p. 300) of Bishop William of March, "In this mans time [1293—1302] the chapter-house was built, by the contribution of well-disposed people; a stately and sumptuous worke." Godwin wrote, I suppose, from local tradition, as there is nothing like it in the Canon's history in Anglia Sacra. His date quite falls in with the Professor's extracts.

(53) The Early English fragments which have been built up in the chapel in the Vicars' Close, as well as those which are lying about in the undercroft of the chapter-house, can hardly fail to belong to the destroyed east end. Yet the fragments in the Vicars' chapel agree rather with the style of the west front than with that of the other parts of the church; and they agree with the fragments built into the rectory-house at Wookey (now called, without any reason, Mellifont Abbey), which can hardly fail to have been parts of Jocelin's house there. The fragments in the undercroft have the tooth-moulding, which, I think, is not found anywhere else in the church, though it is in the undercroft of the chapter-house.

As for the actual form of the east end, it is plain that it was not an apse, nor yet a square east end of the full height, like York, Ely, and Southwell. It will be seen on the ground-plan that the aisles of Jocelin's work run a bay to the east of the site of his high altar. This shows that there was a procession-path and most likely a chapel beyond it on the site of the present presbytery, though it is possible that it ended in a mere retrochoir, like that at Abbey Dore, or that carried round the northern apse at Peterborough.

(54) The church of Glastonbury is, I need not say, of far more ancient foundation than that of Wells; it was its junior simply as a cathedral church. Bath is immeasurably older than Wells as a city, and as a church also, if we accept the foundation of Osric in 676. Even the foundation of Offa in 775 comes before Wells had gained any importance. See Monasticon, ii. 256, though it is hard to understand how a monastery could be destroyed by Danes before the time of Offa.

(55) Angl. Sacra, i. 564. "Hic sibi similem anteriorem non habuit, nec hucusque visus est habere sequentem."

(56) Ib. "Tandem defunctus, in medio chori Welliæ honorifice sepelitur." Godwin adds, "He was buried in the middle of the Quier that he had built, under a Marble tombe of late yeeres monsterously defaced."

LECTURE III.

(1) The story, as given by the Canon of Wells, may be read at length in Anglia Sacra, i. 564, with Wharton's note, and more briefly in Godwin's quaint English, p. 297. It is summed up in the Tewkesbury Annals (Ann. Mon. i. 133): "Magister Rogerus Cantor Sarum eligitur in Episcopum Bathoniæ. Confirmatur a Domino Papâ, non obstantibus cavillationibus Canonicorum Wellensium. Consecratur, intronizatur, et Dominus Rex reddidit ei omnia temporalia, in Junio." This annalist, as a monk, looks on the complaints of the seculars of Wells as "cavillationes."

(2) Anglia Sacra, i. 565. "Unde Episcopus Rogerus in tantum ita instantius penes Papam procuravit, quod ipse pacem fecit inter partes prædictas, et formam apposuit in eorum mutuis electionibus de cætero faciendis, quæ usque hodie observatur."

(3) The chief of these were the *custodia* or wardship of the Deanery, *i.e.* the profits of the decanal estate during a vacancy, which had no doubt hitherto gone to the Bishop as superior Lord, as those of the Bishoprick itself went to the King. He also gave them two-thirds of the profits of all the parish churches in the diocese during their vacancies, which had hitherto gone to the Bishop; the remaining third he gave to the Archdeacons.

(4) Godwin gives the list in p. 298. His burial in the Lady chapel in the cloister has been already mentioned; see above, p. 17.

(5) Anglia Sacra, i. 566. "Ubi ad præsens multis fulget miraculis."

(6) Ib., 567. "Ad cujus tumbam olim multa præclara fiebant miracula." The wonders at the tomb of William of March seem to have ceased when the Canon wrote, while those at the tomb of William Button still went on. This agrees with what Godwin says, p. 299: "Many superstitious people (especially such as were troubled with the tooth-ake) were wont (even of late yeeres) to frequent much the place of his buriall, being without the North side of the Quier, where we see a Marble stone, having a pontificall image graven upon it."

(7) His building of the hall is mentioned in Anglia Sacra, i. 567, as also the advancement of his own family. So Godwin, 299, who speaks of "That goodly hall of the pallace at Welles, pulled downe some fifty yeeres since by a knight of the court, that for a just reward of his

sacrilege, soone after lost his head." This means Sir John Gates, of whom more anon. Robert Burnell was first Treasurer and then Chancellor of England, and in 1278 was elected Archbishop of Canterbury, but the election was annulled by Pope Nicolas IV. In Rymer's Fœdera, vol. i. part ii. p. 559, will be found a letter of Edward I. to the Pope on behalf of his Chancellor. He speaks of the "fidelitatis suæ constantia quam ad recolendæ memoriæ dominum, Henricum Regem Angliæ, illustrem genitorem nostrum, et nos ac totam ecclesiam Anglicanam semper hactenus habuit incorruptam, et a quâ nullo umquam tempore nubulo vel sereno flecti potuit seu etiam deviare." He also calls him "vir tam in temporalibus quam in spiritualibus circumspectus, vir mitis, affabilis, vir benignus, vir etiam misericordiæ, mansuetudinis, caritatis, et pacis." Two of his brothers were drowned in 1282, in the Welsh war; see Trivet, p. 305.

On the works of Gower at St. David's, see the History of St. David's, pp. 190—194.

(8) I must again quote Professor Willis, in the Somersetshire Proceedings, xii. 19. "In 1326 a grant of the land at the east end of the Cathedral by the bishop to one of the canons, measures its length of fifty feet eastward from the wall of the *newly-constructed chapel* of the Blessed Mary." This plainly means the Lady chapel at the east end, distinguished as a new building from the older Lady chapel in the cloister. The Bishop is, of course, John Drokensford, Bishop from 1309—1329. In the Bristol report of Professor Willis (p. xxix.) he is strangely called *Tokenfield*, which I am sure is not the Professor's own description of him.

(9) Of the coved or waggon roofs of the West of England and South Wales, which modern church-restorers generally think it such a great feat to get rid of, I have written and spoken till I am nearly tired of the subject. The arch employed is of all manner of forms, but in a wooden construction the semicircular arch has the best effect. A roof of this sort is the same thing in wood which a barrel-vault is in stone, and the vault of the choir at Wells is a barrel-vault, modified by the clerestory windows. Earlier barrel-vaults of Romanesque date, identical in principle with the Somersetshire wooden roofs, may be seen in Saint Sernin at Toulouse and the chapel in the White Tower of London, and, to come nearer home, in the priory church of Ewenny in Glamorganshire.

(10) Somersetshire Archæological Proceedings, xii. 19. "In 1325 the bishop gave half the proceeds of his visitation to the '*novum opus*' of the church at Wells, and an order was made that, because the stalls

were ruinous and misshapen, every canon should pay for making his own new stall, and the dean sent to Midelton for boards to make the new stalls." Midelton is what we now call Milton. The Dean was John Godele, Dean from 1308 to 1333. The Bishop was of course Ralph.

(11) Anglia Sacra, i. 569. "Sepultus in presbyterio ecclesiæ Wellensis inter gradus chori et summum altare in tumbâ de alabastro, cui imago supponitur valde conforma figuræ illius."

(12) Godwin, p. 302. "His body was buried before the high altar under a goodly monument of Alabaster, compassed about with grates of yron. About a 60 yeeres since (for what cause I know not) it was remooved to the North side of the presbytery, but lost his grates by the way."

(13) Somersetshire Archæological Proceedings, xii. 19. "In 1318 receivers were appointed for the tenths, given in aid of the *new campanile*, and for the oblations to Saint William. . . . In 1321 we find a grant from the clergy of the Deanery of Taunton in aid of the roofing of the *new campanile*," meaning, not improbably, a wooden spire. By Saint William is meant Bishop William of March; see p. 107.

(14) Ib., 21. "In 1337 a convocation was summoned to consider, among other matters, the raising of money by the non-residents for paying a debt of 200 li. incurred for the restoration of the greatest part of the fabric. In 1338 another Convocation was summoned, because the church of Wells is so enormously fractured and deformed ('enormiter confracta . . . totaliter confracte et enormiter deformate'), that its structure can only be repaired, and with sufficient promptitude, by the common counsel and assistance of its members." This evidently means, as the Professor explains it, the damage done by the weight of the new tower, and the props which we now see are evidently the result of the repairs then ordered.

(15) The likeness had struck myself independently, but I see that Professor Willis (p. 22) quotes the same name as applied by Leland to the props of the same kind afterwards inserted under the central tower at Glastonbury.

(16) Anglia Sacra, i. 570. "Iste ad constructionem occidentalis turris in parte australi Wellensis ecclesiæ duas partes expensarum apposuit; ac pro vitro occidentalis fenestræ ejusdem ecclesiæ centum marcas persolvit; duasque magnas campanas in dictâ turri australi pendentes fieri fecit propriis sumptibus." Godwin (302) adds to the account of

the bells, "The bigest of which being cast fower times since I was of this church, now at last serveth for the greatest of a ring, the goodliest for that number (being but five) (I thinke) in England."

(17) Godwin, 304. "It is supposed he was a great benefactor and contributor toward the building of the North-west tower at the West ende of the Church, which his armes fixed upon divers places of the same doo partly shew."

(18) "He built our Library over the Cloysters," says Godwin, in his account of Bubwith, p. 304. But I do not see how this is to be reconciled with what he says in the next page; "He [Beckington] built (as to me at least wise seemeth) the East side of the cloyster."

(19) There are others of the kind, the west front of Exeter for instance, where I suppose that most people would allow that the shape is positively unsightly. The earliest English instance I know of was the Romanesque west front of Malmesbury Abbey. It is now in ruins, owing to the fall of the western tower which was afterwards added. But it is easy to make out that the oldest front had a blank wall between turrets, instead of either towers or the natural endings of the aisles without towers.

(20) This arrangement gives the churches of Wells and Rouen a sort of western transept. There is also a western transept at Lincoln and at Peterborough, but it is formed in a different way by a projection beyond the towers.

There is something analogous to Wells and Rouen in the west front at Ripon. The towers are now at the ends of the aisles, but, as they were at first without aisles, they must have been built as a projecting transept.

(21) This custom of a sham gable or other finish between the towers, having no reference to the gable of the nave, is common both in French and German churches. It is carried to its furthest extreme in the churches of Brunswick, where any one coming from the due west would take each church to be nearly double the height that it really is.

(22) I am here speaking of polygonal apses only. In our large Romanesque churches the round apse was commonly used, but their choirs have commonly been altered or destroyed, so that the only round apses that we now have on a very large scale are those of Norwich and Peterborough. In Normandy many more have been preserved, and they are also much more common in smaller churches. Canterbury Cathedral has an apse to the choir of intermediate date, besides the round chapel at the extreme east end, answering in some measure to our polygonal Lady chapel.

(23) The Wimborne arrangement of a central and western tower was once much more common than it is now, but in many cases one of the towers has either never been carried up or has been afterwards destroyed, as at Hereford, Shrewsbury, Malmesbury, Bangor, and Christ Church in Hampshire. The arrangement still remains on a vast scale at Ely, and on a smaller at Purton in Wiltshire and in the two lesser churches at Coutances.

(24) Anglia Sacra, p. 569. " Episcopale palatium apud Welliam forti muro lapideo circumcinxit, et aquam undique circumduxit;" and again, " Palatium episcopale Wellense muro lapideo batellato et cornellato cum fossatis claudere fecit."

(25) Bishop Godwin tells the whole story in his quaint way (p. 301). "This man is famous for the first foundation of our Vicars close in Wels. The memory of which benefit is to be seene expressed in a picture upon the wal at the foot of the hall staires. In it the Vicars kneeling, seeme to request the Bishop in these words:

> Per vicos positi villæ, pater alme rogamus,
> Ut simul uniti, de [te?] dante domos maneamus.
> *Disperst about the towne, we humbly pray,*
> *Together, through thy bounty, dwell we may.*

He answereth them thus:

> Vestra petunt merita, quod sint concessa petita,
> Ut maneatis ita, loca fecimus hic stabilita.
> *For your demaund, deserts do plead, I will do that you crave,*
> *To this purpose established, here dwellings shall you have.*

This picture being now almost worne out; at what time of late yeeres the Vicars by the gratious favour of her Maiesty had their revenues confirmed to them, being in danger to be spoyled of them by certaine sacrilegious cormorants; they likewise caused a picture of excellent workmanship to be drawen, contayning a memoriall of both the one and the other. These buildings being erected; toward the maintenance of some hospitality in them, he gave unto that new Colledge, the mannor of Welsleigh, and allotted them twenty nobles yerely to be paid out of the vicarage of Chew. He built moreover a house for the Queristers and their master."

(26) See above, p. 173.

(27) I must again quote Godwin, p. 306. "To his successor he gave 100*l.*, upon condition he would accept it in lieu of all dilapidations, otherwise willing his executors to spend it in lawe against him: and lastly unto his executors he left onely 20*l.* a piece, requiring them

to imploy all the rest of his goods to good uses at their discretion. They answered very justly, the trust reposed in them, and that with such discretion as well as fidelity, that I should do them wrong not to remember them. The one was Richard Swanne, Provost of Welles and parson of Yevelton, that heretofore had beene executor after the same sort unto Richard Praty Bishop of Chichester (this man dwelt in the cannonicall house that is neere the market place). Another was, Hugh Sugar Doctor of lawe and Treasurer of Welles (he built the chappell all of free stone, which was of wood before, adjoyning to the great pulpit, and dwelt where I now do, in the middle house of the three that joyne upon the Cambray). And the third was John Pope Doctor of Divinity Prebendary of Saint Decumans and parson of Shyre. These three (as I have beene told by old men) lye buried in a ranke together, over against the great pulpit under three marble stones of one fashion. The Bishops goods that remained unbequeathed, they bestowed for the most part, in building the Vicars close at Welles, which had beene begun by Bishop Ralfe long before; a sumptuous and beautifull worke."

(28) Some remarks of Mr. Dimock's on this subject will be found in the Proceedings of the Somersetshire Archæological and Natural History Society, lxii. 33.

(29) At Hereford some of the Priest Vicars bore the title of Minor Canons. I do not know in what they differed from the rest of the body.

(30) He seems not to have done anything for the fabric, though the north-west tower was still unfinished. But he gave tithes and other property to the Chapter for various purposes, one of which was keeping a common table; "ad mensam capitularem et alia onera in ecclesiâ Wellensi supportanda." Anglia Sacra, i. 570.

(31) Anglia Sacra, i. 570. "Fecit etiam construi per executores suos in vico vocato *la Mountarye* mansiones pro xiv capellanis in dictâ ecclesiâ Wellensi indies celebrantibus." Godwin calls it "a colledge at Welles for fowerteene priests, at the ende of the lane now called Colledge-lane." On the history of this foundation, see Monasticon, viii. 1465.

(32) In the account of the Deans in Anglia Sacra, i. 590, we read of him. "Vir impensè literatus, postquam in utrâque academiâ Anglicâ bonis studiis operam dedisset, in Italiam profectus, Guarini Veronensis disciplinæ se tradidit."

(33) See Mr. Parker in the Somersetshire Archæological Society's Proceedings, xi. 144 and xii. 25. Mr. Parker may be implicitly trusted on all architectural points, but he has quite failed to grasp the history of the foundation.

(34) When I wrote this passage and an earlier passage in p. 23, I did not think how near my worst fears were to being accomplished. The organist's house at Wells, more strictly the house of the *Informator Puerorum* (see above, note 25), a house of the fifteenth century, stands to the south-west of the church, and was connected by some smaller buildings with the west wall of the cloister. The north gable, with a singularly elegant window of two lights, formed a striking object in crossing the Cathedral green, and held no mean place among the general group of buildings of which the church was the centre. For a long time past the building had been in a disgraceful state, and a munificent private offer to repair it was, for what reasons no man can guess, refused. Since that time, the buildings which connected the main body of the house with the cloister have been pulled down. This was a senseless act; for, though they had been much patched and mutilated, ancient portions still remained, and, in any case, their presence kept the house in its proper position as part of a whole. At last, on the night of April 12th, 1870, the ancient roof of the house, which still remained, fell in, damaging the gable and shattering the tracery of the window. How this came to pass there is no distinct evidence, but it is believed on the spot not to have been wholly accidental. Thus it is that our antiquities are daily perishing, because, while a taste for them and an appreciation of their value is daily spreading, those whose duty it is to preserve them are often those who have the least feeling for them. In the present case the damage which has been already done is the result of wilful neglect, but the complete destruction of the building would be a further act of wanton barbarism. I am by no means certain that the house could not even now be saved by a careful repair; but even if destruction has gone too far for that, what remains ought to be kept as a well-preserved ruin, and not to be swept away for any frivolous private purpose.

(35) In this point of view the history of Wells is well worthy of the care of students of municipal history. The number of boroughs which arose under the shadow of abbeys, as at Saint Alban's and Bury Saint Edmund's (on which last see Mr. Green's papers, published in Macmillan's Magazine in the course of 1869), is not small; but of *Bishops' boroughs* there are not many. Durham and Salisbury (see above, p. 3) are the nearest examples, but their history is not exactly the same as

that of Wells. Coventry, a still greater city, grew up under the shadow of an Abbey which became a Bishoprick.

(36) Catalogue of Bishops, p. 307.

(37) This was done in the year 1526 by authority of a bull of Pope Clement the Seventh ; see, for instance, the account of Daventry Priory, in Northamptonshire, in the Monasticon, v. 176.

(38) This was in 1414. A list of the houses suppressed is given in the Monasticon, viii. 1652. Among them was the Priory of Stoke Courcy, in our own county, which was a dependency of the Abbey of Lonley in Maine. Most of the estates of these monasteries went to the various foundations which grew up in the fifteenth century, as several of the Colleges at Oxford and Cambridge, the College of Eton, to which Stoke Courcy went, and Saint George's Chapel at Windsor. It should be noticed that this suppression took place under King Henry the Fifth and Archbishop Chicheley, than whom there certainly never was a more religious King or Primate in England. We have here the closest parallel to the disestablishment and disendowment of the Irish Church.

(39) The suppressions under Henry the Eighth were the most complete contrasts to the suppressions under Henry the Fifth. The small portion of the monastic estates which went in any way to the public service, in the foundation of bishopricks and colleges and in providing for the defence of the coast, was a trifle compared with the boundless wealth which was squandered and gambled away among Henry's minions, to say nothing of the wanton and brutal desecration of churches and consecrated objects.

(40) We should always distinguish between the two suppressions of Henry the Eighth's reign. The suppression of the lesser monasteries was done legally by Act of Parliament. The greater monasteries were suppressed by extorting from each Abbot and Convent an illegal surrender, which surrenders were afterwards confirmed by Act of Parliament. But Abbot Whiting never surrendered, so that the seizure of Glastonbury Abbey was simple robbery. The Abbot was of course really hanged for refusing to betray his trust. The nominal charge on which he was condemned by commissioners sent to "try and execute" him—the thing being thus arranged beforehand—was a ridiculous pretence of his having robbed the goods of the monastery, that is, having tried to save them from those who wished to rob them. This should be borne in mind, as I have seen it said over and over again that the Abbot

was hanged for denying the King's supremacy, which the Abbot and Convent of Glastonbury, like other Abbots and Convents, had acknowledged long before.

(41) See above, p. 46.

(42) The list of Deans in Anglia Sacra, i. 590, says, "vir laicus, decanatum Wellen-em ab anno 1537 pessimo exemplo tenuit. Capite plexus est 1540. 28. Julii."

(43) See Hook's Lives of Archbishops, viii. 18.

(44) Saint George's Chapel at Windsor was not suppressed; otherwise the few collegiate churches which still survive, including those of Ripon and Manchester, which have become cathedral, were refounded under Elizabeth and James the First. It was now that Beverley and several other great churches, as well as some smaller ones, like Stoke-sub-Hamdon in our own county, ceased to be collegiate.

(45) The deed of pretended exchange is printed in the Monasticon, ii. 294. See also Godwin, p. 311; and Collinson's Somersetshire, iii. 395.

(46) It was now that the Palace at Wells was restored to the Bishoprick. After the execution of Somerset it had passed to Sir John Gates, the destroyer of Stillington's Lady chapel, who was beheaded along with John Dudley, Duke of Northumberland, in 1553. He is the knight of the court, of whom Godwin speaks in his account of Bishop Burnell.

(47) On the history of the so-called Priory, see the Monasticon, vii. 664.

(48) See note 44.

(49) See above, p. 50.

(50) See Godwin, p. 311.

(51) This strange document, dated in 1592, has, as far as I know, never been printed, and I have only seen an English translation. It first recites the doubts as to the legal position of the Chapter, arising out of the surrender made by Dean FitzWilliams in the time of Edward the Sixth, and the consequent establishment of a new Deanery by Act of Parliament. The Queen then founds the cathedral church anew, with all its dignities and prebends as they existed before. She then

goes on to found "certain other dignities or offices," namely those of the Canons Residentiary. The names of the existing Residentiaries are recited, and the Dean and Canons Residentiary are constituted a corporation, by the title of the "Dean and Chapter of the Cathedral Church of Wells." To this newly-founded corporation the Queen grants the cathedral church, its appurtenances and movable goods, the Chapterhouse and other lands and property, namely such as had been the common property of the Chapter. She then grants to them power to make, under certain conditions, statutes "for the good rule, government, and ordering of the Canons Residentiary and *other Prebendaries* in the said Cathedral Church." She then prescribes the number of Residentiaries, who are not to be fewer than six nor more than eight, and the manner of their election. They are to be chosen from the Prebendaries, a strong preference being given to the Dignitaries, including the Archdeacons, and the Dean having a right to a Residentiary's place if he chooses to claim it. The term of residence is fixed at four months at least yearly for a Dignitary being a Residentiary, and at three months at least for a Residentiary not being a Dignitary. These, it will be remembered, are exactly half the terms of residence fixed by Jocelin; see above, p. 90. The document then goes on to regulate the visitatorial powers of the Bishop, which are taken for granted. Then follow grants to the different Dignitaries and Prebendaries of their several corpses, and provision is made for the payment of certain customary sums to the fabric, the Vicars, and other purposes. Then come the names of the existing Prebendaries; and it is ordered that the Prebendaries "shall for ever be joined and combined with the aforesaid Dean and Chapter and their successors, to the ends, intents, and purposes following only, that is to say, the Prebendaries aforesaid, every of them and their successors, and the successors of every of them, shall have a stall in the choir of the Cathedral Church aforesaid, and that they and every of them shall have a place and voice in the Chapter of the said Cathedral Church only to elect a Bishop to the Episcopal See of Bath and Wells aforesaid, whenever it shall be needful." The Bishop's right of appointing to dignities and prebends is then renewed, saving only that the right of appointing to the Deanery is reserved to the Crown. The remaining provisions are merely formal.

The evident object of this document is to legalize a certain state of things which had gradually grown up by abuse. It had probably become customary for the non-resident Canons to be summoned to meetings of the Chapter only when a Bishop was to be elected. They were now formally deprived of their right to vote at other times. The Dean and Residentiaries, who had hitherto been simply certain of the Canons or Prebendaries selected for a certain purpose, were now themselves made the corporation, and the corporate style of Dean and Chapter was transferred to them. From this some grotesque results follow. The Chapter is first of all defined as a body of which the non-residentiary Canons are not members, and then the non-residentiary Canons are defined to be members of that body for one particular purpose ; and the old formula, according to which each Canon had "vocem in capitulo et stallum in choro," is preserved, with the restriction that the voice is to be used only at the election of a Bishop. Then the practice by which the consent of the existing Residentiaries was needful for any Canon to keep valid residence is stiffened into an actual election by the existing Residentiaries. Lastly, the custom by which the Chapter always elected a nominee of the Crown to the Deanery is changed into an actual nomination of the Dean by the Crown. In all these cases the object is to legalize by royal authority an existing vicious practice.

It is curious to mark how, in the teeth of all this, some ancient customs are still retained as matters of form. The Canon, on his first appointment to his prebend, is solemnly installed in choir and chapter-house, but no such ceremony follows on his election to a residentiaryship, when he is simply put in possession of a house. This is of course because, under the older state of things, the Residentiaries were not a distinct body, but simply those among the Canons on whom the duty of residence fell on behalf of the whole. When a Canon began to reside, he was not invested with any new office; he therefore needed no new installation. By the Elizabethan Charter the Residentiaries were changed into holders of distinct dignities or offices, but no form of installation was prescribed, or could be prescribed, because the Residentiary retained the stall which he held before, and had no special stall as Residentiary. With the careless modern practice of Residentiaries or other Canons occupying stalls which belong to others of their brethren neither ancient order nor the Elizabethan Charter has anything to do.

It is worth noticing that in the list given in Collinson's Somersetshire, of the Chapter as it stood in his time, the Dignitaries and Prebendaries are all put in their proper order, with the words "Canon Residentiary" added to those who happened to be so. It is now the fashion to print the Residentiaries first in larger type, and the other Canons after them in smaller type. Such are the straws which show the way of the wind, and thus does oligarchy grow in all times and places.

(52) The actual rights of the non-residentiary Canons, both at Wells and elsewhere, is a question of law, to be settled by a legal examination

of various local statutes and general Acts of Parliament. The result would probably not be exactly the same in every church. But it is certain that, if our capitular bodies are to be of any use at all, they must be restored to their old broad basis. A body of forty or fifty clergymen, the pick of the diocese, partly resident at the cathedral, partly elsewhere, might be trusted to do many things which an oligarchy of four or five cannot be trusted to do. In the New Foundations the object would be gained by giving votes in Chapter to the Honorary Canons.

(53) It would hardly be believed, except that the same havoc has been wrought in some other churches, that in an English cathedral church, in the year 1869, four stoves of incredible ugliness were set up, *with chimneys driven through the vaulted roof!* For the better display of one of them, part of Bishop Beckington's canopy, already moved from its place, was cut away; but, on the coming into residence of a Canon of better taste, it was put back. If the church wanted warming, the object might surely have been gained in some other way. In Bristol Cathedral there are stoves which are no disfigurement whatever.

(54) They would, however, have a precedent in the famous scene between Archbishops Richard and Roger in the time of Henry the Second, which I will describe in the words of Godwin, p. 51. "At the time appointed the Legate came and tooke his place, and the Archbishop of Canterbury sate him downe next unto the Legate upon the right hand. After this in came Roger Archbishop of Yorke and would needes have displaced Canterbury to sit above him: that when the other would not suffer, he sate him downe in his lap. The other Bishops present, amased at this strange behavior of the Archbishop of Yorke, cried out all upon him; the Archbishop of Canterburies men by violence drew the other out of his ill chosen place, threw him downe, tare his robes almost from his backe, trode upon him, beate him, and used him so despitefully, as the Legate, whether for shame or for doubt what might happen to him selfe in such a tumult, got him out and went his way."

On the tomb of the doer of this havoc is written, with an unconscious sarcasm, "Multum ei debet ecclesia Wellensis." The words seem happily borrowed from Lucan's address to Nero:

"Multum Roma tamen debet civilibus armis,
    Quod tibi res acta est."

Dean Jenkyns, however, did not employ fire; the stoves were reserved for the next æra.

(55) There is much in the details of the work at Llandaff which is fairly open to censure, but the principle of arrangement is thoroughly good throughout, and the general effect is admirable.

(56) It is proposed to "restore," as it is called, the west front at a cost of many thousand pounds, while there are no signs of any movement towards getting rid of the crying abuses in the inside of the church. I believe there is no fear of the wanton destruction of any of the ancient work, or of any such absurdities as putting up new statues. Still it seems to me to be a strange putting of the cart before the horse to spend such a sum, or indeed to spend a single farthing, on purely ornamental work, while the arrangements of the inside are such that the church does not properly fulfil its first duty as a place of worship. When the nave of Wells Cathedral is again applied to its proper use, it will be time enough to think of canopies and carved work on the outside. And I am by no means clear that purely ornamental work of this kind ought to be restored at all. Anything that is really needed for the safety of the fabric should be done with all boldness, and all really essential features should be made good. If the western towers were likely to fall, it would be a matter of duty to support or to rebuild them, as the case might call for. And as the doors and windows are essential parts of the building, I should without scruple restore their decayed bases, mouldings, and other portions. But as to the purely ornamental work, the statues and their canopies, it seems to me that their value comes wholly from their being genuine parts of the original work, and that any modern repair is out of place. I should take every means to preserve them and keep them in their places; but, if they fall or crumble away, I should not replace them. I therefore greatly regret, on every ground, to see a work undertaken which can hardly fail to have the effect of putting off the real restoration of the church of Wells for many a day.

(57) If the screen is, which I do not believe that it is, of any constructive use in keeping up the piers of the eastern arch of the tower, the obvious thing is to build a fourth Saint Andrew's cross in the eastern arch as in the other three.

INDEX.

A.

Abbeville Collegiate Church, west front of, 125.
Abbey Dore, east end of the church, 177.
Adalbero, Archbsp. his changes in the Church of Rheims, 32, 165.
Adam of Domersham quoted, 170.
A eliza of Löwen, wife of Henry the First, 43.
Ælfsige detains lands of the Bishoprick, 29.
Ælfsige, last Abbot of Bath, 36.
Æthelm, first Bishop of Somersetshire, 26.
Alby Cathedral, absence of transepts in, 116.
Alexander, third Dean of Wells, 170.
Alien Priories, suppression of, 147.
Amiens Cathedral, its great height, 116.
Andrew, Saint, his wells, 19; yields to his younger brother, 36.
Angers, undercroft of the Bishop's palace at, 176.
Apses, various kinds of, 130 their rarity in England, 130; use of, in Romanesque times, 181; more common in Normandy than in England, ib.
Archdeacon of Wells, ancient house of, 142; its alienation, 110; recovery of the other property of, 150.
Archdeacons, their rights under the charter of Elizabeth, 188.
Architects, employment of professional, in the middle ages, 81.
Athelney, prebend attached to the Abbey, 83.
Augustine, his mission to Britain, 12.
Avalon, of Glastonbury.
Axe, the English frontier in 597, 13, 17.

B.

Bangor Cathedral, arrangement of towers at, 182.
Banwell, history of the lordship, 27, 29, 31; Bishop's house at, 37.
Barlow, William, Bishop, alienates the lands of the see, 149, 166; partly recovers them, 149.
Bath, its Roman origin 13, 36; taken by the West-Saxons, 36; church of, founded by Offa, 36, 177; monks brought in by Eadgar, ib; burned, 36, 47; bought by Bishop John, 36, 37, 166; see of Somersetshire removed to, ib.; church rebuilt by Bishop John, 37; settlement between the Churches of Bath and Wells, 45; suppression of the Monastery, 46, 148; restoration of the Church in the seventeenth century, ib.; works of Bishop Robert at, 46-48, 167, 168; date and style of the present church, 48; monks of, illegally elect Bishop Roger, 105; gradually neglected by the Bishops, 107; form of the west front, 125; alleged foundation of Osric, 177.
Bath and Wells, origin of the title, 10, 45.
Battle Abbey, lofty undercroft under the dormitory, 176.
Bayeux, installation of the Bishop at, 158.
Beaufort Cardinal, enlarges the Hospital of Saint Cross, 163.
Beauvais Cathedral, remains of the old church at, 79, 80; its great height, 116.
Beckington, Thomas, Bishop, works of his executors; his various works, 145; removal and mutilation of his canopy, 152; his work in the cloisters, 181; his will, 182, 183; his gifts to the Chapter, 183.
Benefice, meaning of the word, 59, 169.

Berengar, agent of Archbishop Thomas, 173.
Beverley Minster, compared with Wells, 124, 130; unreality of its west front, 128; east end of, 130; compared with Wells, 132.
Bird, Prior, his works at Bath, 48.
Bishop, his share in the daily distribution, 174; his right of visitation saved by the Elizabethan charter, 187; election of, under the charter, 187, 188.
Bishops, their relations to their cathedral churches, 10, 11, 45; difference between their position in England and elsewhere, 12; their ancient territorial style, 12; how appointed in early times, 25; Norman and French Bishops after the Conquest, 35; number of, increased by Henry the Eighth, 53; their greater power in the old cathedrals, 54; plunder of, under Edward the Sixth and Elizabeth, 149.
Bishopricks moved from small towns to larger, 35, 166.
Bishopstool, meaning of the word, 12.
Boniface the Ninth, Pope, his bull about entertainments, 175.
Bourges Cathedral, absence of transepts in, 116.
Bourne, Gilbert, Bishop, recovers the lands of the see, 149.
Bridgewater, more modern than the other Somersetshire towns, 14.
Bristol, Church of St. Mary Redcliff, internal effect of height in, 133.
Bristol, position of the Cathedral, 2; harmless stoves at, 189.
Brunswick, sham fronts in the churches of, 181.
Bubwith, Nicholas, Bishop, his share in building the north-west tower, 122; his gift of the Guild-hall to the citizens, 123; his buildings in the cloister, *ib.*
Bury Saint Edmund's, its municipal history compared with Wells, 184.

C.

Canon, title of, not to be confined to the Residentiaries, 50; meaning of the name, 51.
Canons, honorary, unknown in the old foundations, 140.
Canons, non-residence of, 89; their share in the daily distribution, 174; their three sources of income, *ib.*
Canons residentiary and non-residentiary, origin of the difference, 85 et seqq.
Canterbury Cathedral, propping of the central tower at, 119; its double apse, 182.

Carlisle Cathedral compared with Wells, 134, 135.
Carol, see Karole.
Cathedral Churches, their clergy sometimes regular, sometimes secular, 21; distinction of old and new foundations, 53; foundations under Henry the Eighth, *ib.*; held to be the freehold of the Chapter or Convent, 64; urgent need of their reform, 160.
Cathedral, meaning of the word, 8-10.
Century, thirteenth, its special historical importance, 103; fourteenth, character of its architecture, 111, 113.
Chancellor of the Church, foundation of the office, 59, 168; its duties, 57.
Chancellor of the Diocese distinguished from Chancellor of the Church, 57.
Chantries, suppression of, 149.
Chantry Priests, incorporated by Bishop Erghum, 141, 142, 183; suppressed, 142, 150.
Chapter-House, different character of, in regular and secular churches, 96; building of that, at Wells, 96-98, 176; polygonal type of, 97; style and date of, at Wells, 98; examples of the polygonal shape, 176; of the oblong shape, *ib.*
Chapters, origin of, 21; their relation to their Bishops, 45; their increased independence of the Bishops, 63, 64; need of their reform on the old basis, 189.
Chartres Cathedral, its great height, 116.
Chester Cathedral, crumbling nature of its stone, 135.
Chester, position of the Cathedral, 2; foundation of the Bishoprick, 53.
Chew Magna, pension from the vicarage to the Vicars of Wells, 182.
Chicheley, Archbishop, his character, 185.
Chichester Cathedral, fall of the spire at, 117.
Choir, meaning of the word, 78; its original extent at Wells, *ib.*; in Somersetshire churches often unworthy of the nave, 80; practice of lengthening in the thirteenth century, 108; change in the site at Wells, 110; recasting of clerestory and triforium, 111; character of the roof, 112; objectionable arrangements of, at Wells, 155, 167.
Choristers, house of, see Organists' house.
Christ Church, Hampshire, arrangement of towers at, 182.
Chrodegang, Bishop of Metz, his rule for canons, 32, 165.
Cities, their greater importance on the Continent than in England, 12.
Clement the Seventh, Pope, his bull for the suppression of monasteries, 185.
Cloister, difference of, in regular and secular churches, 83; date of that at Wells,

83, 84; needed in a monastery, but not in a secular church, 31, 32.
Cloister, originally of wood, 84; Lady chapel in, rebuilt by Bishop Stillington, 144; original building of, 172; orders of Chapter about, *ib*.
Close wall, destruction of, 143.
Cnut, King, his favour to Bishop Duduc, 26, 28.
Collegiate Churches, meaning of the word, 10; suppression of, 149.
Collinson's History of Somersetshire, its misrepresentation of the story of Harold and Gisa, 27; list of canons in, 188.
Combe, bought by Gisa, 31; Prebends of, 51, 60.
Congé d'élire, meaning of the word, 16, 164; distinguished from the letter missive, 25, 164.
Congresbury, fabulous Bishoprick at, 14; history of the lordship, 28, 29.
Corporate Isolation, spirit of, its effects, 62.
Corps, meaning of the word, 51.
Coventry Cathedral, canons substituted for monks at, 173.
Coventry, apse of Saint Michael's Church at, 130; crumbling stone used in the church of, 135; origin of the city, 185.
Coventry and Lichfield, joint Bishoprick of, 46; destruction of the Church of Coventry, 64.
Crediton, see of, removed to Exeter, 35.
Cromwell, Thomas, Lord, his share in the suppression of monasteries, 147; holds the Deanery of Wells, 148; enforces the payments of Residentiaries, 175.
Crypt, see Undercroft.
Cynewulf, spurious charter of, 15, 164.

D.

Daventry Priory, suppression of, 185.
Dean, foundation of the office, 50, 168; how appointed in various churches, 54; its duties, 55, 56; effects of its foundation, 63; office at Wells held by Thomas Cromwell, 148; estates alienated under Edward the Sixth, 150, 168; re-endowed and the old estates recovered, 150; rights of, under the charter of Elizabeth, 187; appointment of, transferred to the Crown, 188.
Deaneries held by laymen, 148.
Deanery House built by Dean Gunthorpe, 142.
Dignities, origin of, 50, 168; duties of, 55-57; difference among, in different churches, 60.

Dimock, Mr., 77; quoted, 140, 183.
Domesday, its account of the lands of the Church of Wells, 33, 166.
Dorchester, Bishoprick of, 163.
Drokensford, John, Bishop, deed of his quoted, 179.
Duduc, Bishop of Somersetshire; his favour with Cnut, 26, 28; his bequests to his church, 28; a Saxon by birth, 165; his tomb, 166.
Dunstan, Saint, builds the stone church of Glastonbury, 24, 164.
Durham, analogy of its history with that of Wells, 3.

E.

Eadgar, King, brings in monks at Bath, 36.
Eadgyth, wife of Eadward the Confessor, her grants to Gisa, 31.
Eadward the Confessor, his favour to Bishop Duduc, 26; his grants to Gisa, 31, 165; introduces the Norman style into England, 48; his church at Westminster the great model, 69.
Eadward the Elder founds the Bishoprick of Somersetshire, 13.
Ealdhelm, first Bishop of Sherborne, 164.
Early Gothic Style, two forms of, in Wells Cathedral, 74—77; peculiar character of, in Somersetshire and South Wales, 75.
East Ends, various kinds of, 130.
Edward the Sixth, act of, for the suppression of colleges and Chantries, 142, 149; robbery of ecclesiastical bodies under, 148.
Elizabeth, Queen, her charters to the Vicars, 140; to the Chapter, 151.
Ely Cathedral, style of, 75; loss of the spire at, 129; east end of, 130; size of the triforium, 134; arrangement of tower at, 182.
Embezzlement, various instances of, 39.
Ergham, Ralph, Bishop, incorporates the College of Chantry Priests, 141, 142.
Eton College receives lands of Alien Priories, 185.
Evercreech, Bishop's house at, 37.
Evesham, its parliamentary rivalry with Wells, 4-5, 163.
Ewenny Priory, roof of the Church, 179.
Exeter, history of the city and Bishoprick, 2, 35; Bishop Leofric's changes at, 33; history of the Deanery of, 54; loss of the spires at, 129; form of the east end, 130.

O

INDEX.

F.

Fitz-Williams, Dean, surrenders the estates of the Deanery, 186.
Fontanenses Episcopi, Bishops of Somersetshire, so known at Rome, 45.
Frederick Barbarossa, Emperor, his dispute with Pope Hadrian the Fourth, 169.

G.

Gates, Sir John, dismantles the hall of the palace, 179; beheaded, 186.
Gerent, King of Cornwall, defeated by Ine, 164.
Gervase, historian of Canterbury, quoted, 172.
Gisa, Bishop of Somersetshire, his quarrel with Earl Harold, 27-29, 165; his birth in Lorraine, 30; increases the revenues of his church, 31; makes his canons follow the rule of Chrodegang, 31-33; his buildings, 33.
Gisa, his gifts to the canons, 33; his death and burial, 34; his account of the Old-English church, 67.
Glastonbury, its whole history gathers round the Abbey, 3; permanence of the British Monastery at, 18; its original wooden church, 19, 164; stone church of Dunstan, 24; annexed to Bath by Savaric, 70, 71; formed part of the style of the Bishops, 70, 71; again separated from Bath and Wells, 71; surrenders estates to Jocelin, 71; style of the Early Gothic of the Abbey, 75; cloister of wood, 84; goodness of the stone at, 135; suppression of the Monastery, 147; destroyed by Edward, Duke of Somerset, 149; relation of the Bishops to, 171; antiquity of the foundation, 177; central tower propped as at Wells, 178.
Gloucester Abbey, vault in, built by the Monks' own hands, 81, 172; west front of, 125.
Gloucester and Bristol, joint Bishoprick of, 46.
Godele, John, Dean, his share in repairing the choir, 180.
Godfrey, Bishop of Bath, his birth in Lower Lorraine, 43; his character, *ib*.; he tries to recover the canons' lands, *ib*.
Godwin, Bishop, his catalogue of Bishops quoted, 28, 56—57; 113-134.
Gower, Bishop, his works at Saint David's, 179.
Green, Mr. J. R., quoted, 165, 170, 184.
Grey of Wark, Lord, preserves Wells Cathedral in Monmouth's rebellion, 4.

Grosmont, Monmouthshire, state of the church at, 8.
Gunthorpe, John, Dean, builds the Deanery, 142, 183.
Gwent, meaning of the name, 17, 164.

H.

Haddan, Mr. A. W., quoted, 173.
Hadrian the Fourth, Pope, his dispute with the Emperor Frederick, 169.
Harewell, John, Bishop, his share in building the South-west Tower, 122.
Harold, Earl, his quarrel with Bishop Gisa, 27, 29, 165; his writ as King to Gisa, 165; Gisa's view of his death, *ib*.
Henry the First, his charters to John de Villulâ, 36, 37; his opposition to Bishop Godfrey, 43.
Henry the Third, character of his reign, 105; promotes the illegal election of Bishop Roger, 106; his grant to the Church of Wells, 172.
Henry the Fifth, suppression of monasteries under, 147.
Henry the Eighth, character of his reign, 145-147; suppression of monasteries under, 147; enforces the payments of Residentiaries, 175.
Henry of Blois, Bishop of Winchester, holds the Abbey of Glastonbury with the Bishoprick, 44; helps Bishop Robert in his reforms at Wells, 52.
Hereford Cathedral, loss of the spire at, 129; character of the east end, 130; loss of the western tower, 131; position of the Vicars and Minor Canons at, 140, 141; present good arrangement of, 158; choir screen at, 159; its arrangement of towers, 182.
Hermann, Bishop, joins the sees of Sherborne and Ramsbury, and removes the see to Old Sarum, 31, 165.
Hildebert, Provost, embezzles the property of the canons, 39, 166.
Historiola de Primordiis Episcopatûs Somersetensis, quoted, 28, 47.
Honorary Canons, proposed extension of their rights in the new foundations, 189.
Howden Collegiate Church, octagonal Chapter-house at, 176.
Hugh, Bishop of Chester, substitutes canons for monks at Coventry, 173.

I.

Ilminster, lost prebend of, 174.
Ine, his victories over the Welsh, 14; founds Taunton, *ib*.; probably founds the

INDEX.

church of Wells as collegiate, 15; defeats Gerent of Cornwall, 164; founds Taunton, *ib.*; his laws, *ib.*
Innocent the Fourth, Pope, corruptly confirms the election of Bishop Roger, 106.
Installation of Canons, 188.
Isaac, Provost of Wells, 33, 166.

J.

Jenkyns, Dean, his doings in the Cathedral, 189.
Jocelin of Wells, his episcopate, 70; his style during the union with Glastonbury, 71; his compromise with Glastonbury, *ib.*; his works at Wells, *ib.*; his banishment, 72; his special connexion with the church and city, *ib.*; first founder of the Vicars, 72, 84; extent of his building, 74-76; his domestic works at Wells and Wookey, 76; consecrates the church, 77, 174; character of his works, 78; how far the designer of the church, 81; probable nature of his relations to it, *ib.* increases the dignities and prebends, 84; his statute of residence, 90, 174; his position among the Bishops of Wells, 104, 177; destruction of his tomb, *ib.*
John de Villulâ, first French Bishop of Somersetshire, 35; buys the town of Bath and removes the see thither, 36, 37, 166; his government and buildings at Bath, 37, 166; his oppression of the Canons of Wells, 37, 38; builds himself a house at Wells, *ib.*, 166.
John, Provost and Archdeacon, his dealings with the canons, 39, 166; his repentance, 49.

K.

Karole, meaning of the word, 172.
King, Oliver, Bishop, his works at Bath, 48.

L.

Lady, proper title of a West-Saxon King's wife, 31.
Lady Chapel, character of, at Wells, 109; date of, 179.
Lady Chapel in the cloister, 83.
Leases for three lives, early cases of, 61.
Lee, Roland, Bishop of Coventry and Lichfield, tries to save the Church of Coventry, 64, 170.
Le Mans, Cathedral of, 69; its date, 100.
Leofric, Bishop, his changes in the Church of Exeter, 33; moves the see of Crediton thither, 35.

Letter missive, see Congé d'élire.
Lichfield Cathedral, apse of, 130; east end compared with Wells, 132; present good arrangement of, 158; choir screen at, 159; octagonal Chapter-house at, 176.
Lincoln Cathedral, style of, 75; said never to have been consecrated, 77; residence kept by the dignitaries at, 92; effect of lowness in the inside, 116; loss of the spires at, 118, 129; unreality of the west front of, 125, 128; arrangement of the east end, 131; effect of lowness in the interior, 133; octagonal Chapter-house at, 176.
Llandaff Cathedral, style of, 75; no Residentiaries ever founded at, 85; west front of, 125, 126; present good arrangement of, 156-158, 190; system of Prebendaries and Vicars, 17; the Archdeacon President of the Chapter, 169; form of the Chapter-house, 176.
Long Sutton, lost prebend of, 174.
Lorraine, or Lotharingia, meaning of the name, 30; canonical rule of, 32.

M.

Malmesbury Abbey, original west front of, 181; arrangement of tower at, 182.
Manchester, collegiate church becomes cathedral, 16; suppressed and restored, 186.
Margam Abbey, octagonal Chapter-house at, 176.
Mark granted to the Church of Wells by the Lady Eadgyth, 31.
Mary, Queen, property of the Church recovered under, 149, 150.
Master of the Fabric, office of, 5-7.
Master, technical use of the name, 88.
Matthew Paris, his account of the Church of Westminster, 170; of the earthquake at Wells, 171; of the consecration of various churches, *ib.*
Mendip, its early state, 17.
Midelton or *Milton*, timber fetched from, 180.
Minor Canon, title unknown at Wells, 140; use of, elsewhere, 183.
Monasteries, suppression of, 21; effects of, at Ely, Peterborough, and elsewhere, 22.
Monks, original character of, 20.
Monmouth, James, Duke of, doings of his followers at Wells, 4.
Morganwg, meaning of the name, 17, 164.
Mounterye, College of, see Chantry Priests.
Muchelney prebend attached to the Abbey, 17.
Mudgeley, granted to the Church of Wells by the Lady Eadgyth, 31.

N.

Nave, proper place for the congregation, 154, 155 ; plea for its proper use at Wells, 157-160.
New Foundation, Cathedral Churches of, meaning of the name, 53 ; greater influence of the Crown in, 54.
Nicolas the Fifth, Pope, his bull about payments made by Residentiaries, 175.
Non-residence, origin of, 58 ; growth of, 87.
Non-residentiary Canons, origin of, 89 ; value of the class, 89, 90, 150 ; defrauded of their rights at Wells by the charter of Elizabeth, 151 ; retention of their rights at York, 152 ; their position under the Elizabethan charter, 187, 188 ; general question as to their rights, 189.
Norman Architecture, spread of, after the Conquest, 67.
Norman Conquest, its effects on the Church, 35.

O.

Offa, King of the Mercians, founds the Church of Bath, 36.
Old Foundation, Cathedral Churches of, meaning of the name, 53 ; closer connexion of the Bishops with, 54 ; general likeness of their constitutions, 66, 85.
Old Saint Paul's Cathedral, loss of the spire at, 129 ; minor canons of, 140.
Old Sarum, see Salisbury.
Organist's House, foundation of, 182 ; neglect and ruin of, 184.
Osbern, his life of Saint Dunstan, quoted, 164.
Ottery Saint Mary, spire of lead remaining at, 129.
Oxford, position of the Cathedral, 2 ; foundation of the Bishoprick, 53.

P.

Pagan, origin of the name, 11.
Palk, Sir Lawrence, his championship of Wells against Evesham, 163.
Pakington, Sir John, compared with Saint Dunstan, 5, 163.
Parker, Mr., house restored by, 68 ; quoted, 129, 183.
Payne of Pembridge, claims the Provost's estate, 60.
Perpendicular style, its characteristics in Somersetshire, 121, 122.
Pershore Abbey, apse of, 130.
Peterborough Cathedral, the west front an addition, 76 ; its perfection, 125.

Petty Canons distinguished from Priest-Vicars, 140.
Pluralities, early instances of, 44 ; causes of, in the Middle Ages, 5-8.
Pole, Reginald, holds two Deaneries as layman, 148.
Pope, John, Prebendary, executor of Bishop Beckington, his works, 138.
Prebendaries, become corporations sole, 65 ; their exempt jurisdictions, *ib.*
Prebends, origin of, 50, 168 ; meaning of the name, 51 ; their position, 52 ; refounded by Elizabeth, 187.
Precentor, foundation of the office, 50, 168 ; its duties, 56.
Priest-Vicar, title of, 139.
Provost, origin of the office, 33 ; becomes hereditary, 39, 166 ; suppression of the office, 150.
Purton Church, Wiltshire, arrangement of tower at, 182.

R.

Ralph of Shrewsbury, importance of his episcopate, 108 ; his place of burial, 113 ; his connexion with the eastern reconstruction, 114 ; fortifies the palace, 137 ; founds the College of Vicars, 137, 182 ; portions of his work remaining, 138 ; treatment of his tomb, 177.
Ramsbury, poverty of the church of, 31.
Reformation, the, its real character in England, 145, 146.
Reginald, son of Hildebert, restores the canons' lands, 49 ; appointed precentor, 60, 167 ; withstands the claims of his nephews, 6.
Reginald, Bishop, founds new prebends, 70.
Regular Clergy, their distinction from the seculars, 20.
Residence, Jocelin's regulations as to, 90 ; devices to hinder, 91.
Residentiaries, origin of, 89 ; number not originally fixed, 90 ; their number and mode of appointment, 92 ; growth of their powers, 93 ; necessity of their constant residence, 94, 95 ; their encroachments by virtue of the charter of Elizabeth, 151, 152 ; necessity of their residence, 152 ; great entertainments required of, 175 ; commuted for a payment, *ib.* ; use of entertainments restored, *ib.* ; their new position under the Elizabethan charter, 188 ; not installed, *ib.*
Restoration, principle on which it should be carried out, 190.
Rheims Cathedral, its great height, 116 ; grandeur of the doorways at, 127.
Rheims, Church of Saint Remigius at, 69.
Rib, meaning of the word, 91, 138.

Richard, Archbishop of Canterbury, story of, 189.
Richard of the Devizes, his account of the non-residence of canons, 86, 173.
Richard of Tittenhanger, monk of Saint Alban's, designs buildings in the Abbey, 171.
Ripon, collegiate church becomes cathedral, 16; suppressed and restored, 186; its west front, 181.
Robert, importance of his episcopate, 40; becomes Bishop of Bath, 43; of Flemish descent, but born in England, 44, 167; his early history, *ib.*; represents Bishop Henry of Blois at Glastonbury, 44, 167; settles the controversy between Bath and Wells, 45; his works at Bath, 46, 48, 161; he recovers the lands of the canons, 49; founds the dignities and prebends, 50, 52, 167; increases the number of canons, 57, 162; his description of his objects, 61; his buildings at Wells, 66-69; single fragment of them remaining, 68; grants North Curry to the Chapter, 190; grants municipal rights to the city, *ib.*
Robert, Bishop of Hereford, present at the consecration of Robert's church at Wells, 68.
Robert Burnell, Bishop, his place in the history of England, 107, 179; his works at Wells, 108.
Robert Grosseteste, Bishop of Lincoln, his dispute with his Chapter, 170.
Roger, Archbishop of York, story of, 189.
Roger, Bishop, elected by the monks of Bath only, 105; confirmed by Innocent the Fourth, 106, 177; his gifts to the canons of Wells, *ib.*; last bishop buried at Bath, 106.
Roger, Bishop of Salisbury, opposes Bishop Godfrey, 43.
Roger Witing, claims the Provost's estate, 60; cf. 170.
Romanesque style of architecture; its character, 48.
Roofs, character of, in Somersetshire, 112.
Rouen Cathedral, analogy of its west front to that of Wells, 127.
Rouen, Saint Ouen's Abbey Church at, union of French and English merits in, 117.

S.

Saint Alban's Abbey, work at, designed by a monk of the House, 81; arrangement of the Lady chapel at, 131; its municipal history compared with Wells, 184.
Saint Cross, Hospital of, its title, 163.
Saint David's, constitution of the Residentiary body at, 93; absence of a Dean at, 169; history of, compared with Wells, 176; works of Bishop Gower at, 178.
Saint Quentin Collegiate Church, its great height, 116.
Salisbury, analogy of its history with that of Wells, 3; origin of the Bishoprick, 31; style of, 75; the spire constructively a mistake, 118; mode of propping, 119; unreality of the west front of, 125, 128; its doorways compared with Wells, 127; octagonal Chapter-house at, 176.
Savaric, Bishop, attaches prebends to two abbeys, 68; unites the church of Glastonbury to the see of Bath, 70, 78.
Saxon, meaning of the name, 26.
Screens, close, an abuse in secular churches, 157.
Screens, open, their good effect at Lichfield and Hereford, 159.
Secular Clergy, their distinction from the regulars, 20.
Serel, Mr., quoted, 170, 175, 177.
Sham Fronts common in France and Germany, 181.
Sherborne, foundation of the Bishoprick, 13; division of the diocese, *ib.*; see removed to Old Sarum, 31; Ealdhelm, first Bishop of, 164.
Shrewsbury Abbey, arrangement of towers at, 182.
Sinecure, meaning of the word, 55.
Slymbridge Church, Gloucestershire, style of, 75.
Somerset, Edward, Duke of, appropriates the lands of Wells and Glastonbury, 149.
Somersetshire, mainly Welsh in 597, 13; lack of any central town, *ib.*; picture of, in the time of Ine, 16, 17; gradually becomes English, 18; local architecture of, 48; Early Gothic style of, resembles French work, 75; characteristics of the Perpendicular style in, 121, 122.
Southwell, Chapter house at, 97; changes in the west front at, 128; loss of spires at, 129; form of the east end, 130; compared with Wells, 131; no President of the Chapter at, 176.
South Wales, likeness of its Early Gothic to that of Somersetshire, 75.
Spires, often covered with lead, 129.
Stalls, each canon makes his own, 113; wrong arrangement at Wells, 153.
Stephen, King, helps Bishop Robert at Wells, 52, 168.
Stillington, Robert, Bishop, rebuilds the Lady chapel in the cloister, 144; destruction of his tomb, *ib.*
Stoke Courcy Priory, suppression of, 185.
Stoke-sub-Hamdon College suppressed, 186.
Stone, early use of, in building, 23.
Stoves, intrusion of, at Wells, 153.

Sub-Chanter, foundation of the office, 50, 57; its suppression, 150, 168.
Sub-Dean, foundation of the office, 50, 57, 168; its property and jurisdiction, 65, 168.
Sugar, Hugh, Treasurer, executor of Bishop Beckington, his works, 138.
Sumorsætas, give their name to Somersetshire, 12; obtain a Bishop of their own, 13.
Supremacy, Royal, accepted by both regular and secular clergy, 146.
Swan Inn laid open to the Cathedral, 143.
Swan, Richard, Provost, executor of Bishop Beckington; his works, 138.

T.

Taunton, founded by Ine, 14, 17, 164.
Tewkesbury Abbey, apse of, 130.
Tewkesbury Annals quoted, 178.
Theological College, proposal for its union with the Vicars' College, 139; position of its officers, 169.
Thomas of Canterbury, Saint, his life quoted, 87.
Toulouse, roof of the church of Saint Sernin at, 179.
Towers, Old-English, character of, 24; central, a peculiarly English and Norman feature, 115; absence of, in the great French churches, 116.
Treasurer, foundation of the office, 50, 168; his duties, 57.

U.

Undercroft, under the Chapter-house, 97, 176; other instances, *ib.*

V.

Vicars' Close, first built by Ralph of Shrewsbury, 138; recast by Beckington's executors, *ib.*; modern changes in, 139.
Vicars, origin of, 84; account of, by Richard of the Devizes, 86, 173; story of a vicar at Saint Paul's, 87, 173; their original duties, 89; lived originally in the canons' houses, 87, 138; Jocelin's legislation about, 88; incorporated by Ralph of Shrewsbury, 137; change in their position consequent on the institution of residentiaries, *ib.*; their petition to Ralph, 138; building of the Vicars' Close, *ib.*; their collegiate manner of life, 139; question as to its possible restoration, *ib.*; distinction between vicars and petty canons, 140; admission of laymen to the college, *ib.*; distinction between lay-vicars and singing-men, 141; charter of Elizabeth for their share in the distribution, 174; property given them by Ralph, 182; payments secured by the charter of Elizabeth, 187.
Vitalis, Vicar at Saint Paul's, 173.

W.

Waltham, mode of life of the Canons, 164.
Wardship, meaning of, 178.
Wedmore, granted to the Church of Wells by Eadward the Confessor, 31; prebends of, 51.
Wellesley, manor of, granted to the Vicars, 182.
Wells, Chapter of, its original foundation, 14, 15; older than the Bishoprick, 15; original number of the canons, 24, 39; increased by Gisa, 31; their original manner of living, *ib.*; compelled to live together by Gisa, 32, 33; their first property distinct from the Bishop, 33; oppression of, by Bishop John, 38; embezzlement of their property by the Provosts, 39; breaking up of Gisa's discipline, 40; settlement of the controversy with Bath, 45; becomes the sole Chapter under Henry the Eighth, 46, 148; property restored by Reginald, 49; new constitution of under Bishop Robert, 49-52; nature and use of the different offices in, 54; increase in the number of canons, 57; connexion with the Bishoprick weakened through Robert's changes, 62-64, 173; part played by in the dispute with Glastonbury, 71; its constitution fixed by Jocelin, 72; distribution of its revenues, 90, 174; regulations as to residence, 90, 174, 176; origin and number of residentiaries, 92; their mode of appointment, *ib.*; rules as to their residence, 94; grants of Bishop Roger to, 106; untouched by the suppression of monasteries, 148; lands lost by and recovered by Bishop Bourne, 150; charter of Queen Elizabeth to, 151, 186; its effect on the relations of the two classes of canons, 151, 152, 187; its rules as to residence, 176, 187; its new foundation of the Chapter, 186; held to consist only of the Dean and Residentiaries, 106, 188; inconsistency of the new system, 188.
Wells Cathedral Church, its general effect as compared with other churches, 5; always a church of secular canons, 6, 8; founded as a collegiate church by Ine, 15; becomes cathedral under Eadward the Elder, 16; analogy of Ripon and Manchester, *ib.*; character of the oldest building, 24; tombs of the early bishops,

26; works of Bishop Robert in, 66; long retention of the old English church, 66-70; consecrated by Robert, 67; character of his building, 68, 69; beginning of the works of Jocelin, 71; lectures of Professor Willis on, 72, 73; extent of the work of Jocelin, 74; two styles of Early Gothic in, 74-76; date of the west front, 76; fall of the vault and consequent repairs, 76-77; its arrangement and appearance under Jocelin, 78-79; breaks and stoppages in the nave, 79, 80; its condition at the end of the thirteenth century, 98-100; gradual reconstruction of its eastern portions, 103—114; addition of the Lady chapel, 109; changes in the choir and presbytery, 100-112; its completion in the fourteenth century, 114; raising of the towers, 115-123; dangerous state of the central tower, 118; the danger remedied by props, 119-121; finishing of the western towers, 122; position of Wells among English churches, 124, 136; essentially a second class church, 124; criticism on the west front, 125-128; excessive smallness of its west doors, 126; lack of finish to the Western towers, 129; character and special beauty of the east end, 130—132; marked horizontal lines in the nave, 132, 133; treatment of the Arcades, 133, 134; little damage suffered by, 135; excellence of the stone, 135; its connexion with the surrounding buildings, 136; the church and its appurtenances, completed in the fifteenth century, 145; modern changes in, 152; objectionable arrangements in, 153-156; necessity of reform, 157-161; Henry the Third's grants to, 172; fragments of the older east end, 177; its probable form, ib.

Wells, Historian of, known as the *Canon of Wells,* quoted, 28, 47.

Wells, Palace of, built by John de Villulâ, 37, 166; its original position, 38; present building built by Jocelin, 76; its style, 76, 81; great hall added by Robert Burnell, 108, 178; moat and wall added by Ralph of Shrewsbury, 137, 162; alienated to Edward Duke of Somerset, and recovered, 149, 186; undercroft in, 176; the hall dismantled by Sir John Gates, 177.

Wells, peculiar character of its history, 1-4, 143; its interest purely ecclesiastical, 3; relations of the city to the Bishop, *ib.*; parliamentary rivalry of Wells and Evesham, 4, 163; general effect of its buildings, 5, 6; the oldest seat of the Somersetshire Bishoprick, 11; why chosen as such, 14; contrast with Glastonbury, 19; origin of the name, 19; preservation of ancient buildings at, 22, 136; destruction of ditto, 23, 142, 143; never a walled town, 36; position of, under John de Villulâ, 37; grant of municipal rights by Bishop Robert, 40; analogy of its history with that of England, 101-104; practically restored to its old position, 106; gift of the Guildhall by Bishop Bubwith, 123; grant of municipal rights by Bishop Robert, 170; interest of its municipal history, 184.

Wells, Saint Cuthbert's Church, its peculiar constitution, 4; disproportion of its nave and choir, 80.

Wells, Saint John's Priory not a monastery, 150; its suppression, *ib.*

Welsh, their position in Somersetshire, 17.

Westminster, history of the Church of, 53, 170; Norman Church of, the great model in the twelfth century, 69, 170; octagonal Chapter-house at, 176.

West-Saxons, their conversion to Christianity, 13; their first Bishoprick, *ib.*

Whitchurch Church, style of, 75.

White Tower, roof of the chapel in, 179.

Whiting, Richard, Abbot of Glastonbury, his martyrdom, 61; its cause, 147, 185.

William, Abbot of Saint Alban's, his works, 171.

William Button the First, Bishop, his nepotism, 107; consecrated at Rome, 171.

William Button the Second, Bishop, his holiness, 107; alleged miracles in his tomb, *ib.*

William Fitz-Stephen, quoted, 173.

William of Malmesbury, quoted, 35; his account of the Church of Westminster, 170.

William of March, Bishop, alleged miracles at his tomb, 109; oblations at his tomb, 171.

William of Sens, architect of Canterbury Cathedral, 172.

William of Wykeham, designs the nave of Winchester, 81.

William the Conqueror, his grants to Gisa, 31.

William the Englishman, architect of Canterbury Cathedral, 172.

William Rufus, grants the Abbey of Bath to John de Villulâ, 36; sells the town to him, *ib.*

Willis, Professor, his lectures on Wells Cathedral, 72, 73; his opinion of the date of the west front, 76; of the Chapter-house, 98, 176; of the Lady chapel, 110, 179; his remarks on central towers, 118, 180; his account of the choir, 113; of Glastonbury, 164.

Wimborne Minster, grouping of towers at, 131, 182.

Winchester Cathedral, nave of, designed by William of Wykeham, 81; west front of, 125; arrangement of the Lady chapel, 129.

Winchester, foundation of the Bishoprick, 13, 163; division of the diocese, *ib.*

Windsor, Saint George's Chapel, receives lands of Alien Priories, 185; escapes at the suppression of Colleges, *ib.*

Winesham, history of the lordship, 29, 31.

Wolsey, Cardinal, his suppression of monasteries, 147.

Wookey, Bishop's house at, 37; its connexion with the Sub-Deanery, 65, 168; Jocelin builds the manor at, 76, 171; its style, 76, 81, 177.

Worcester, plan and date of the Chapter-house, 176.

Wormestor, or Worminster, lands at, bought by Gisa, 31.

Wrexham Church, apse of, 130.

Y.

Yatton Church, disproportion of its nave and choir, 80.

York Minster, burning of, 47; residentiaries at, how appointed, 92; chapter-house at, 92; architecture of the nave, 111; west front of, 125; grandeur of its doorways, 127; arrangement of the east end, 131; loss of height in the nave, 133; position of the Vicars at, 141.

THE END.

R. CLAY, SONS, AND TAYLOR, PRINTERS, BREAD STREET HILL.

www.ingramcontent.com/pod-product-compliance
Lightning Source LLC
Chambersburg PA
CBHW031813220426
43662CB00007B/632